Uphill All the Way

Uphill All the Way

How You Can Lose Weight, Gain Confidence, and
Become a Successful Entrepreneur Through
QVC and the Lite Bites® Fat-Fighting System

MARVIN SEGEL

NEWMARKET PRESS
NEW YORK

FIRST EDITION

10   9   8   7   6   5   4   3   2   1

Library of Congress Cataloging-in-Publication Data:

Segel, Marvin.
    Uphill all the way: how you can lose weight, gain confidence,
    and become a successful entrepreneur through QVC and the
    Lite Bites® Fat-Fighting System/Marvin Segel.
        p. cm.
    ISBN 1-55704-387-6 (hc)
    1. Segel, Marvin. 2. Overweight men—United States
    Biography. 3. Businesspeople—United States Biography
    4. QVC (Firm) 5. Reducing diets. I. Title.
    RM222.2.S398   1999
    613.2'5—dc21
    [B]   99-23860
                                                        CIP

Quantity Purchases

Companies, professional groups, clubs, and other organizations
may qualify for special terms when ordering quantities of
this title. For information, write Special Sales Department,
Newmarket Press, 18 East 48th Street, New York, NY 10017,
call (212) 832-3575, or fax (212) 832-3629.

Manufactured in the United States of America.

To my father, for the great business values and ethics he has instilled in me. As we have grown older, we have learned to respect each other more than ever.

And to all the Lite Bites® successes who have shared their stories with me and with their fellow QVC viewers. While they may claim that Lite Bites and I have changed their lives, it is they who have inspired me and given meaning to mine.

Acknowledgments

E sther Margolis, publisher of Newmarket Press, planted the idea in my head that I could write this book when she visited QVC in connection with Suze Orman's book. Without her encouragement, this book might never have happened. Although other publishers jumped on the bandwagon, Esther tucked me under her wing from the start, and I liked what she and Newmarket Press are about. To her I owe a big thank you!

Two writers helped me prepare the manuscript for publication. Jack Engelhard, the author of *Indecent Proposal*, helped me with the initial draft. We were a contradiction in terms, but he helped this book get its start.

At Esther's suggestion I met Susan Schwartz. From the moment we talked, we hit it off. Susan pulled more of the details out of me and gave the book its final polish. She also helped me with some personal issues that came up during the final draft and was there for me when I needed some emotional support.

I also want to thank . . .

All the great people at QVC who think of me as "The Lite Bites Man," or just Marv. I cannot tell you how good that makes me feel. Being Joe Segel's son can be cool for a while, but of course I want to be known for what I've done, not what my father's done. I have made lots of friends at QVC, and they are my friends because I'm Marvin Segel. I really do appreciate them.

Dean and Cheryl Radetsky, who put their heart and soul into creating Lite Bites. Without their genius, we'd all probably still be on yo-yo diets . . . or worse. Their dedication and insight into helping improve the lives of all those who struggle with their weight has not only given us Lite Bites, but has empowered us to love ourselves no matter what we weigh.

Finally, the Lite Bites customers. The letters and on-air calls make me feel great. We all have down days at times. All I have to do is read some of the mail that comes in or listen to the talking photo cube one on-air guest, Cathy Palmeri, gave me, to pick myself back up. Cathy went from a size 22 to a size 2 using the Lite Bites Fat-Fighting System. Other viewers have contacted me with similar results. Their comments and their successes have inspired me and make everything I do worthwhile, including this book.

It is a great feeling to make it on your own and have the respect and friendship of others.

Thank you!

Contents

Uphill All the Way

Introduction

Luck, Timing, and Life

Welcome to QVC, the world's premier electronic retailer, and welcome to my life. By the way, QVC stands for Quality, Value, Convenience. Today, my life *is* QVC, on which I'm the national spokesperson for Lite Bites Fat-Fighting products, used by tens of thousands of QVC viewers. Making QVC my life should have been so simple, since it was my dad, Joseph Segel, who founded the world's largest electronic retailer in 1986. I wish it had been that simple; you have to know QVC and my dad.

Some might expect any boss's son to be welcomed into the family business with fanfare. That did not happen with QVC or some of the other businesses my dad started. (He also founded the Franklin Mint 22 years earlier.) For me, it was uphill all the way. In fact, after initially being rejected, it took over a year for Lite Bites to be accepted by QVC—even though Dad was the one who introduced me to the product. Dad, you see, has always been hesitant to mix family into some of the larger businesses he founded. As a very young man and at every step after that, I was faced with the challenge of making it on my own under the shadow of an extremely successful entrepreneur. Yet, this same entrepreneur, by his example, gave me many of the qualities that allowed me to define success on my own terms and achieve it. I salute him for that and am deeply grateful.

In this book, I stay clear of abstract theories on life and business and intend to speak to you heart to heart, in plain language, sharing with you my ups and downs. Through my personal voyage, you will listen in on a three-part adventure that I hope will help you make changes in your life as I did in mine—all for the better.

For this book is indeed three stories in one.

First, you'll read my personal drama in striking out on my own—time and time again—and what I've learned about luck, timing, and life that might help you achieve your own dreams.

Second, I'll share with you the easy, four-step program I followed to achieve a healthy lifestyle through my discovery of Lite Bites and the Lite Bites Fat-Fighting System. Lite Bites products, as you'll learn if you don't already know, were developed by Dean and Cheryl Radetsky and are available only through QVC. In fact, it's the second most re-ordered product on the air. The products, whether they're Lites Bites bars, or wafers, or shakes, or the new and very popular Chewies, contain a special combination of herbs and other nutrients to provide support in a weight-loss program. I'll go into a bit of detail in later chapters about how to combine Lite Bites products with the Lite Bites Fat-Fighting System to give you a healthier lifestyle.

And, finally, as a bonus, I'll give you tips and tricks on making it on QVC. (My father named the company. Further on in the book—in chapter 4—I'll explain how he came up with this concept.)

Please note that I am not so ego-driven as to think you want to know all about me. However, as I navigated my way through life, I learned how to redirect my focus, take on new challenges, and eventually achieve success in the dynamic new business of electronic retailing. My intention here is to share with you my personal story, since it is about setting your sights on a goal that you wholeheartedly believe in and letting nothing sway you from achieving it. I will show you through my example and experience that fresh starts are always possible and success may indeed be just around the corner.

LIFE WITH DAD

When asked what my father does, I like to say he professionally retires. I'm not talking about getting paid to put on his pjs and slippers every night. I'm referring to the fact that he is the ultimate entrepreneur, an empire builder, a risk taker beyond what most of us can imagine. He creates big companies, runs them for a while, then sells them to even bigger companies and "retires," only to become bored and start yet another new and completely different company. The cycle then repeats itself.

After my father "retired" from founding and then running QVC, he visited a spa in Hawaii and, upon his return, handed me some wafers. He'd been approached by someone there who was hoping to get a spot on QVC to market her friend's product. "If these wafers work," Dad said to me, "then you might have a good story to tell on the air."

As with most of my interactions with my dad, this one was businesslike. I inherited the emotional genes in our family, probably from my mother. You have to understand that, when this conversation with Dad took place, my six-foot-three-inch frame carried well over three hundred pounds. I was unhappy with my work and was feeling quite stifled in my profession, which, at the time, was real estate. I had just turned 40 and was feeling those first pangs of my youth ebbing away. Conversations with my dad mostly focused on business values and ethics. I've since learned that my relationship with him was not all that different in content than the relationships lots of men have with their fathers, particularly the sons of very successful fathers. Giving me these wafers was his way of reaching out and helping me. Little did he or I know then that he was providing me with an opportunity of a lifetime.

Looking back on that incident, I can honestly say that luck and timing were colliding at that moment in my life, as they had at other times as well. I believe that when these moments come, you must be prepared to recognize them and act on them, work hard, and see where life leads you.

I could have thrown those wafers away and never given them another thought. I never had any real desire to go before the cameras at QVC and sell anything, even though I was an experienced marketing and sales professional in the real estate business. Yet, these wafers were a link to my father and a chance to prove myself to him, and this seemed to be one of those moments in our life together when he was going out of his way to help me. Little did we know how much these wafers would change my life. On some level I wanted to maintain the connection, to please him, and to report back to him whether these wafers actually worked.

I tried the wafers my dad handed me and, since they tasted good, ordered more from the manufacturers who, as I later found out, were a young entrepreneurial mom-and-pop operation on the West Coast. Within six weeks I'd lost 12 pounds. I was amazed, because I had made no other changes in my life. I had NOT started an exercise program. I hadn't counted a calorie or a carb. I don't even remember eating less than I usually did during that period of intense professional frustration. Yet those 12 pounds came off and stayed off. At this point, I had a checkup with my doctor. I was still very overweight, and my cholesterol and triglycerides were at dangerous levels. I mentioned the wafers that I thought had created the weight loss. My doctor hadn't heard of them and didn't know how they worked, but figured they couldn't hurt me. He urged me to keep eating them.

And so I did.

Now, four years later, after shedding 80 pounds, I'm the national spokesperson on QVC for the Lite Bites Fat-Fighting System. From these rather dry but remarkably effective wafers, the Radetskys developed many different products—yummy bars, shakes, and Chewies among others —made with the same ingredients that help promote a healthier lifestyle, products that QVC viewers reorder to the tune of three hundred thousand Lite Bites bars every month! Was that the result of luck? It would seem so. Here's my dad, founder of QVC, handing me the wafers, and, presto, I'm on the air. But that's not the way it happened. Not at all. In fact, between the first bite and first on-air appearance was a long, torturous uphill battle that I had to overcome. I had to deal with the ups and downs that came with the territory of living out your life to try and make the most out of it.

If you'd like to know how I did it, read on. It takes a bit of explaining, but you might find in the details some answers to questions you've been struggling with in your own life.

Part One
My Personal Story

Chapter One

Being the Boss's Son Doesn't Mean a Special Place to Park: Childhood and the Franklin Mint

I want to make it clear that I love my father, although I cannot remember the last time we said that to each other. But being the boss's son is not an easy role for many children to play. I've since learned we have a typical father-son relationship. I mean, 45 years ago men weren't allowed in the delivery room when their wives were in labor, so a father did not become connected to family life at the moment when the couple became a family. A lot has changed; a lot has not. As I've gotten older and more secure about my own professional role in the world, I understand the forces that drove my father a lot better than I did when I was young and floundering. Today we respect each other's successes more than ever. But that's now—and my understanding of him was long in coming. Not because of who he is, but because of who I was and the struggles I went through to get where I am today.

Now, how did I become so overweight? Simply put, I was unhappy with my life and had been so since I was a kid. My parents divorced when I was nine years old, and I saw my dad one day a week. That day was Sunday and it never varied. Sometimes those visits seemed like an interference for me because as I grew older, there were some Sundays I wanted to stay home and play with my friends. Sometimes Dad had to work on Sundays when I was there. I didn't blame him particularly. Work is what dads of his generation did, or so I thought. Ironically, I was divorced from my first wife when our daughter was about the age I was when my parents divorced, and I vowed I would do things differently with her. But as my career took off and I got busier and busier, I found myself falling into some of the same work traps when my daughter, Devon, visited.

It's not much of a stretch to figure out why I took comfort in food. I was always a big kid who had a good appetite. In elementary school and middle school, I didn't have a lot of friends because I was kinda nerdy, not with computers the way kids can be today, but with gadgets. I was always the first kid with a new gadget—a calculator, a slide rule—and I always knew how to use it. I spent quite a bit of time by myself. Occasionally I'd get picked on because my low self-esteem was pretty apparent. Once or twice I got beaten up by the kids at school.

By high school I weighed over three hundred pounds and, believe it or not, felt okay about it. I had a natural outgoing personality that could withstand a little teasing (well, actually, quite a bit of teasing), and, quite frankly, my bulk gave me a unique identity. I got lots of attention—not all of it good—for being heavier than everyone else, and that attention actually fed on itself (no pun intended). I developed downright bad habits, social quirks that I carried to the extreme, and it took a while for me to break out of that cycle of bad behavior. Part of my personality is that when I do something, I tend to take it to the extreme, so some of my behavior wasn't appropriate for a high-school-age kid.

It doesn't take a genius to figure out why I acted out in inappropriate ways. I had figured out that negative behavior got my father's attention pretty quickly, so I developed a cycle of bad behavior. While in high school, I bought a car— my first car—that brought lots of attention from Dad. It was a Pontiac Firebird Trans Am, a totally inappropriate car for a teenager at that time, because it was very expensive and too powerful for the kind of driving I had to do back and forth to school. That car got his attention and he started talking to me about the value of money. I argued that I'd earned the money to pay for it (well, actually, I'd been hit by a bus when I was 14 and used part of the settlement money to buy the car) and I could spend it the way I chose. He talked to me about making appropriate choices in any given situation.

I grew up with my mother, who had happily remarried in northeast Philadelphia, which is about as middle class as you can get, far away from the lifestyle my dad had with his wife, Doris, and my stepsiblings, Alan and Sandy. (We are so close, we refer to each other as brother and sister.) I went to Northeast High School. Academics didn't particularly interest me, but, ironically enough, broadcasting did. I developed the school's first radio station. It played over the PA system every day. There I arranged for announcements by students regarding school news, sportscasts and sports updates, social events, and community dates that were of interest to the student body. I even won an award from Temple University. At this radio station, I found a way to express my creativity and my developing interest in business. It would be many years and many career detours before I found my way back into broadcasting.

Despite my early acceptance as a broadcaster, I was not very popular in high school. I wasn't really part of the in crowd. Even though the in crowd paid some attention to me, because of my bulk, it was negative attention that didn't do much for my self-esteem.

There was, however, a plus side to it all. Being one of the heaviest kids in high school made me perfect for the varsity football team. All I did was squat at the line and a linebacker would push me forward to clog up the running lanes. I also made the varsity shot-put team. At three hundred plus pounds, I had no problem tossing a 12-pound shot put. I was so good at this that I set a record, since broken I'm sure, for the longest distance thrown.

I might add that shot-putters have an interesting work-out routine. They walk (they don't run) around the track and eat cupcakes. It's no wonder that I got to be so overweight.

After high school, I did not go straight to college. I'd had a part-time job at a new-car dealership. I wasn't a good student and my low self-esteem made it hard for me to see much beyond that next paycheck, so I opted for a full-time job at the dealership. For the two years I worked there, it was great! I had a new car every year, I had some spending money, and, at that age, what more did I need? I thought this was it!

What I didn't foresee at the age of 19 was the first gas crisis. It was 1974. Those big Buicks died, and so did my job.

Dad tried to be supportive, and he did come to my rescue. He offered me a job as a photographer at the Franklin Mint. The Franklin Mint, the largest private mint in the world, was founded by my father in 1964 soon after he remarried. While reading *Time* magazine one day, he was struck by a picture of people lined up around the block of a government building to buy the last U.S. silver dollars minted. A few days later, he came up with the idea of the National Commemorative Society, a membership organization that would issue a series of proof-quality sterling silver coin-medals commemorating events in American history. He engaged a small private mint to produce the coin-medals. After the very first issue in this series, he felt that the quality was not up to his standards, so he decided to start his own mint. Not only did he found the mint, but at the time he offered me the job, it had grown to be a huge publicly traded corporation, and he was running it as president and CEO. Naturally, I accepted his offer. And thus began my first real-life adventure as The Boss's Son. It would not be my last!

MY LIFE AT THE MINT

Yes, it is good to be the boss's son . . . but you're in a no-win situation with your peers, and, at best, it's a rather mixed blessing.

I remember walking through the doors of the Franklin Mint for the first time and there, in the lobby, hung a huge oil painting of the founder, who looked like he'd been dead for a hundred years. I got chills because that was my father, who was only in his mid-40s at the time and very much alive. Even today, wherever I go in life and particularly when I'm starting a new venture, I can still feel those big eyes staring down at me and daring me to do better.

Dad had always been unenthusiastic to the idea of mixing family and business. He had made it clear to me at the outset that while he was prepared to hire me, he would make sure I was treated as any other employee. The job itself did nothing to challenge my creative impulses. Photography was nothing new to me. Dad had taught me how to use a camera when I was nine or ten years old, and he set me up with my own darkroom in the basement of my mom's house when it was clear I was old enough to know not to drink the developer solutions. I had also worked in high school as a photographer for some local newspapers. I was hired on at the Mint as a catalog photographer, which entailed taking individual photos of single coins. That's what I did all day for weeks and months on end, in a windowless, stuffy dark-room in the basement. I became a mole, blinking at the bright daylight every time I took a lunch hour, coming up to stare at real people who moved and talked and whose eyes were used to the light.

To everyone else, however, I was the boss's son. I was greeted warmly by the company's employees, but there was a catch: They did not think of me as Marvin, but rather as "Joe Segel's son."

Being introduced as Joe Segel's son was pretty cool for a while, but then I started to realize that I had no identity. I was Joe Segel's son, period. That doesn't do much for your self-esteem.

I thought I heard whispers about being groomed for some top job, that I was being taught the business from the ground up (literally!). Nothing could have been further from the truth. In fact, I don't think Dad had anything like that in mind. It seemed to me that to him I was just another employee with the same privileges as everyone else, and maybe even fewer. Dad was all business. His obsession with the details of running a business is second to none—yet I've since learned it's a trait that all the most successful entre-preneurs share and it is what makes their businesses suc-cessful. Dad was no different.

As a career move, my job as the photographer-mole was not exactly a dream come true. A promotion or job change at the Franklin Mint was not in the offing since, first of all, this was not an issue I'd ever discuss with my father. No, I knew the boundaries. To many sons, their fathers seem bigger than life. In my case, that belief was literally true because there was still that huge oil painting of him in the lobby.

So there I was, stuck in the basement in a job that I did not love. However, because I was doing a good job photographing those coins, I was eventually given additional duties outside the building. I was assigned to take pictures of special events, such as special tours of the museum and community activities with senior officers.

Finally, some creativity! Some recognition! One of my photographs, of the Franklin Mint building itself, made its way to the cover of the annual report. Oh, I was so proud!

But all I heard was, "You got that plum because you're Joe Segel's son."

That hurt, and to this day I don't know if that photo got on the cover because it was good or because I was the boss's son. It was not the first time I'd heard a comment like that and it would not be the last, at the Mint and even in my current occupation as a QVC spokesperson and marketing consultant. In any case, from that moment on, I knew somehow, some way I would need to get out on my own, to really find out about my self-worth.

But in the meantime, as a more creative indoor and outdoor photographer, I was now in a different job category in the corporate pecking order, and in my opinion, this placed me in a position for a higher salary. I had different responsibilities now, more responsibilities, with a different job description, than when I'd been hired seven months earlier. I determined that I was due a pay increase. I made my request to my immediate supervisor, as any employee would, who then brought it to the human resources manager.

Just imagine that you're the manager of a human resources department for a large corporation and the CEO's son is asking for an out-of-sequence raise. He'd been at the company only seven months and though he'd been given additional responsibilities, his salary review was still some time off. So, what do you say? After all, he is the boss's son. You'd be uncomfortable, right? The very next day, I got a phone call from Mike Boyd, the senior vice president of the Franklin Mint. (Mike was later to work with my dad at QVC.) I knew instantly that my request had created an awkward situation and a problem for Mike and, ultimately, for me.

That was a challenge I'd always have to confront. Despite my father's tremendous business and financial support along the way, I was pretty much left on my own in regard to shaping a career. I'm not complaining, but the road to my own career success took lots of twists and turns before it straightened out.

Dad is all business all the time. One of his colleagues once told me the story of the time he had to ride in a limo with my dad for two hours to get to an off-site meeting. My dad didn't talk to this fellow the entire trip. He sat there reading newspapers and materials for the upcoming meeting, but uttered not one word of chit chat the entire time they were alone together in the car. Yup, that's my dad.

I'm sure you're getting a clear picture: If I needed approval—for anything, personal or business—I would typically not look to my father. I knew he was proud. He just didn't say it the way I wanted to hear it.

One time I phoned him just to say hello. It was at a later

time when Barry Diller was making moves to buy QVC. I said, "Hi, Dad, what's new?" I meant what's new with him personally. His immediate response was, "You know I can't tell you what's going on." He assumed I was asking what was new with Diller.

Anyway, that's how much Dad is into business. His all-business orientation used to bother me a lot more than it does now, now that I've made peace with who I am and who he is.

Mike Boyd and I both agreed that I should resign. No one in the company wanted to take the matter of my pay raise to my father. Mike and I are still friends today, very much so. In fact, Mike turned out to be the friend and mentor we all need when we're trying to reposition our careers. Clearly, without Mike's support, I would not be on QVC today.

But at the time, he explained that he simply could not honor my request. I had unknowingly and rather innocently created an uncomfortable situation for all concerned. And we both realized these situations would come up again and again. He asked me to resign and I was out!

Often I've asked myself if I'd done anything wrong. I tried to second-guess myself again and again. But what did I know of corporate politics at the age of 19 or 20? I was a kid. And even if I had known the proper procedures and routes to take (I thought I'd acted appropriately, in any case), I was doing a different job from the one I'd been hired to do and should have, at some point, been recognized for it.

As it turned out, leaving the Franklin Mint was the best move I ever made. Ahead were a series of adventures that would test whether I would always be tagged as Joe Segel's son or finally be able to stand up on my own. My year at the Franklin Mint, difficult as it was, turned out to be a wonderful learning experience for me. It would not be the last time I would work in the same company as my father. And with each new experience, I gained a lot in terms of dealing with him and the other people we worked with. The next time I worked closely with him, I would be the captain of a corporate jet. And that came about in a very unusual way.

Chapter Two

Life after the Mint:
College, Burglar Alarms,
then Presidential Airways

How did I get moving after I left the Franklin Mint?

First, I enrolled in Bucks County Community College, where I majored in business and computer science. This was a natural choice since business and "gadgets" run in my blood. I got high grades, which proved to me that my fears of having missed out by not taking the direct road from high school to college were groundless. My business street smarts taught me to think fast on my feet. What's more, it's amazing what plain common sense can do—and that's something too often forgotten on campus or even as we go through life. (It's those people without common sense who so often need the real-life equivalent of the computer "undo" button.)

After college, I was jobless and didn't know where to turn. As I contemplated a return to the business world, I was unsure what exactly my role had been in my demise at the Mint. It was not something I thought I could discuss with my dad.

As I write this, I can hear some groaning from readers who think I'm engaging in self-pity. First, self-pity is not in my bones. I am nothing but grateful and feel nothing but blessed.

When I wonder how people who grew up without my advantages can relate to a man who grew up as I did, I think, whether rich or poor, man or woman, everyone can identify with a young man's struggle to find his place in the fast-paced society that is America. Not only that, but the search for approval from peers and grown-ups is a universal experience that cuts across class lines.

We all need that pat on the back as a sign that we're appreciated. I talk to a lot of people from various backgrounds, and many of them have the same story. They grew up with parents who demanded that they should do more, could do more, and could do it better. The same people also tell me that the lack of emotional support leads to second-guessing yourself and the feeling that nothing is quite good enough. Yes, you did this and you did that—but what about that other thing you didn't do? There's always something you didn't do.

What you're left with as you're growing up is this question: Are you worthy?

The answer is yes! In fact, my intention here is to show that anyone can make it. The kinds of experiences that changed my life for the better can change yours as well. There's no time for self-pity. It's time to believe in yourself and get moving! I've said it before and I'll say it again in these pages: I believe in luck, timing, and life. I believe that you prepare for any eventuality and, when the time is right, you too will be able to create your own luck and improve your life.

Just at the time I got out of school, my father was considering buying another business. It wasn't the most exciting business, but when he asked me if I wanted to be involved in it, I said yes. I was grateful for the opportunity to work with him again, this time in a small, family-owned business, rather than in a large, publicly owned corporate entity. We started the Sentrex Protection Systems business in Philadelphia. Sentrex sold and installed wireless burglar and fire alarm systems, the first such systems to be marketed in the area. I was not exactly working for my father, but I got his attention by having to relay the usual kinds of information that backers want: sales units and numbers, marketing efforts and results, stuff like that. Even though he backed the enterprise, I ran the show and I was beginning to realize that I was able to connect with him through business, not through any personal turmoil or joy I may have been experiencing. The impact of that realization was yet to hit me, because I'm an emotional guy by nature and he is not. But on a business level, his advice and support have been unfailing. After about two years of my running this small company, we realized that the "up" side of this business was limited, and we decided to get out of it.

At the time, my father had a new passion. While he was serving as Chairman of the Board of Governors of UNA-USA (United Nations Association of the U.S.A.), he had the occasion to charter a private jet to ferry a group of UN officials and congressmen to a UN conference. That was his first experience with a corporate jet, and he was disappointed with the quality of the plane. So, being the perfectionist that he is, he decided to start a higher quality charter flight service. Within a few months, Presidential Airways was born, starting off with five Citation jets and three Gazelle helicopters. Just at the time the burglar/fire alarm business was winding down, Dad called me and suggested that I learn to fly, with the possibility that I might qualify to become a co-pilot with Presidential Airways.

I jumped at the chance. Once again, I felt that Dad needed me! I could be someone he could trust up there in the cockpit to tell him how things were really going. For me, I would rise from photographer-mole to pilot—from life in a basement darkroom to the wild blue yonder—in a very short time. Actually, I had never before given any thought to learning how to fly a plane, but I wasn't about to turn down this latest offer from Dad. I figured, how hard could it be? It would not be the only time I made such a daring leap into an unknown profession.

So off I went to pilot training school in Ardmore, Oklahoma, at a former military base. There, for one very intensive month, I spent mornings in a classroom and afternoons in the cockpit. It was a rigorous training period, but learning to fly was right up my alley, challenging every talent I possessed. Remember—I love gadgets. Give me a box with a set of instructions and I've got everything figured out in no time. So the plane's instrument panel, for me, was a piece of cake. And I was blessed with very good eye-hand coordination.

I remember one afternoon in the cockpit when the instructor put a hood over my head so that I couldn't see the ground or anything else except the instrument panel. The test was to figure out exactly where the plane was by matching frequencies from two different radio beacons. I took the readings, then pointed to the precise spot on the map where I thought the plane was. Yes, the instructor nodded, I knew exactly where the plane was. He was somewhat amazed. This kind of orientation in the air takes most pilots a lot more training to figure out.

In due course, I became one of the youngest pilots to be certified by the FAA to fly three different jets—a Lear jet, a Citation, and a Westwind—and two helicopters as captain in the cockpit. It was unusual in those days—this goes back 20 years or so—to be certified to fly helicopters by instrument, but I got that classification as easily as I got my jet pilot's standing. I was thrilled.

Becoming a pilot for Presidential Airways, a private charter company operating out of Northeast Philadelphia airport, had other advantages. Not only did I get to meet a lot of celebrities who used our services, but at last I got up from under the stigma of being the boss's son. Yes, my dad owned the company, so technically I worked for him. But I was a pilot and I possessed skills that only other pilots have, not businessmen and numbers crunchers. I commanded respect by the very nature of my work, and I believe I was a very good pilot, too.

My experiences as a pilot taught me some very valuable lessons applicable to the world of business, particularly the fast-paced no-second-chance life I would discover at QVC.

There is no "undo button" in the cockpit, as there is on a computer. You must always plan ahead when you're speeding along at 500 miles an hour. In fact, you're not thinking about those 500 miles—but about the 500 miles ahead. The saying among pilots is: You're either ahead of the plane or behind the plane. And, as pilot, you never want to be behind the plane you're flying.

When you're behind the plane you're in trouble. A snowballing effect takes place when events happen that you haven't prepared for.

For example, when you're taking off from New York's JKF airport en route to Philadelphia, you're already thinking about your landing.

Or, to be more specific, let's say you're at Wilmington, Delaware's airport and you sight a flock of birds dangerously in your path just as you've passed the critical speed, known as V-1, which means you can no longer stop in the remaining distance of the runway. What do you do?

Well, that's exactly what happened to me, and it sure did test my training and my ability to think fast. I was already at a speed of 160 miles an hour and decided to rotate the airplane for takeoff prior to Vr (the rotation speed at which you take off and start the climb), and instituted an immediate sharp turn.

While I was doing this, I started to get the stick shaker—which is the plane's most dramatic warning signal telling me the wing is about to stall and the jet could fall from the sky. I was in this gray area of the performance envelope of the airplane, but my only chance was to make the turn.

I rotated early and instituted a sharp turn because months earlier I had read an article in a pilot's magazine on avoiding bird strikes. The article mentioned that a bird's only defense against being hit—it doesn't want to hit you, either—is to fold its wings and dive.

So I knew my only chance was to climb quickly. The sharp turn was some defensive mechanism inside me that said if I used this technique, I would also be protecting one engine from ingesting any birds.

This whole thought process happened in less than a second, about the amount of response time you get at QVC while doing a show live.

Another time, one of our jets slid off a runway at an airport in New England during a blinding snowstorm. The airport had to shut down until the jet could be removed from the snowbank it was embedded in. As assistant director of operations, I took charge of the situation. I gathered together a couple of mechanics and a Philadelphia flight crew, loaded a twin-engine Piper Aztec with a section of landing gear and a wing flap that would fit the stuck plane, and made the mistake of calling my mother to tell her where I was off to.

She is a typical mother, demanding to know why I had to fly in this kind of weather. One plane was already stuck. Why risk another one's getting caught? My explanations that the plane I was flying was a different kind of plane with a different weight fell on deaf ears. And I must admit, to most people, this seemed like a dangerous thing to do.

But I learned that, if you are well prepared and know what you are doing, as I felt I did, there really is no problem about setting out to accomplish your goal. I must admit the flying was challenging that day. The plane took off from Philadelphia in zero visibility, and I had to rely solely on instruments for the entire trip. I took off by looking only at the center line underneath my front wheel—and the instrument panel, of course. The mission required lots of concentration throughout, and it was a strange feeling to land the Aztec over the Presidential Airways plane that was stuck in the snowbank, but in fact all went very smoothly and we were able to dislodge the plane and reopen the airport. Just to tell you how heavy the snowfall was, the inside of the Aztec's passenger cabin was full of snow the next morning when we boarded. Of course the cabin was shut and locked overnight, but the snow was so intense and so fine, it had penetrated the doorframes.

Did I act foolishly in making this journey? I didn't think so at the time and I don't think so now. I was fully prepared for the challenge and the flight was actually uneventful, which is exactly the way a pilot likes it to be.

Meanwhile, let me tell you about what was happening on the ground. Here I am an accomplished pilot—but I'm still the boss's son. Up in the air I'm the one in control. Down on the ground, at times it's still a very different story.

One day when Dad was a flight passenger he found some stale cookies on board. In spite of the fact that I was the assistant director of operations and a skilled pilot licensed to fly all those different jets and helicopters, Dad wrote me a memo after he landed. It stated, "I want you to taste all the cookies to make sure they're fresh each week." As I've said, attention to detail is the hallmark of an entrepreneur.

This was a job only the boss's son would get. Being the official cookie taster of Presidential Airways naturally had its light side. Besides the usual jokes, someone made up a plaque with my name and official title on it, and above it was a rubber Cookie Monster! But the duties also had its heavy side too, as this particular "expansion" of my duties expanded my waistline as well.

Working for your family, as you can imagine, is very tricky. Either you accept a job beneath your capabilities and work your way up—a long, tortuous route, where you're never sure if you're getting ahead because of your merit or because of who you know—OR you are given a plum assignment and everyone else in the company resents you. It's a no-win situation, one that I have discussed with my business friend Brian Roberts, whose father started Comcast, today one of the country's largest cable companies and owner of several sports teams.

Our situations are somewhat parallel, but the experiences we've had are different. Whenever we met for lunch, we would discuss those differences. Brian was taught the Comcast business from his father's knee. He was invited to sit in on board meetings when he was a youngster, not to participate, but to listen. You can learn a lot by just listening. It was clear that Brian was being groomed from a very early age to succeed his father in business. I envied him. To this day, Brian maintains a close relationship with his dad, who continues as chairman while Brian serves as president of Comcast.

In contrast, my dad had usually been cool to the idea of mixing family and business. Therefore, I had to find my own road, even when I worked for him. Brian and I—though each of us the son of a powerful and entrepreneurial father—were raised under very different circumstances. We took different paths, but we both agreed that we each made the right choices for ourselves.

I am grateful to Dad for the entrepreneurial spirit and solid business values he instilled in me. I have observed him closely and absorbed much of the business wisdom I saw him employ on a daily basis.

People automatically assumed that I had special privileges, that I was being groomed for a top job, the way Ralph Roberts was grooming Brian. Comcast, the first cable company to carry QVC's signal and invest in QVC, now owns a controlling interest in QVC. Comcast began as a cable service provider and now has grown, under the Roberts' leadership, to own many other companies.

The situation at Presidential Airways was different in respect to my relationship with my father. I loved to fly and thought I was going to be doing it my whole life—no, not being the official cookie inspector; I mean being in the airline business. I had tasted the joys of being in control of all kinds of situations. I thought I had found my true calling. Being a pilot for Presidential Airways was like a dream job come true. I didn't even think of it as a job. I thought of it as my career. It was a perfect situation vis-à-vis Dad. No one could dispute my qualifications for my job. I was a good pilot, and I proved it each and every day.

Then Dad, being Dad and true to his entrepreneurial spirit, sold the company.

There's a saying in the airline industry that the way to make a small fortune is to start with a large fortune. Yes, the family lost a lot of money in the airlines, so Dad got out of the business and cut his losses.

I actually stayed on for a while, but it was very different working for a larger, less personal organization. I didn't get choice flight assignments the way I did when the company was small. I did not have to taste the cookies anymore, and, strange as it seems, I missed that, not because I enjoyed being a cookie taster, but because of the personal connection I had with the operations. All that was gone.

So, after a few months, I resigned. I guess I did have a bit of my father's business instincts in me. One of his great strengths is that he knows, after he's built a business, when it's time to move on. It's what keeps his creative juices flowing. Somehow I knew that my days as a pilot were over. It was time for me to move on and develop a different career path, one that would challenge me in different ways. As it turned out, my next venture was a career in real estate.

Chapter Three

Real Estate, Innovation, and Thinking Outside the Box

A fter I left Presidential Airways, I floundered for a bit and then asked my dad for some business advice, which was always sound. His father had been in real estate, so he suggested that perhaps that might be an avenue for me to explore.

I took the bait: I studied, got my real estate license, and plunged in. Although I grew to have no great love of the real estate industry as a whole, I have spent the bulk of my career there (so far!) and enjoyed gratifying success in that business.

Again, I attribute my success to luck, timing, and life. I believe that people are given opportunities every day—I call those opportunities "luck"—and with that luck comes the implicit demand that we change. An opportunity presents itself, and it demands that we change our lives in order to take advantage of it. Some people are good at recognizing those lucky breaks and some are not. Why? Because luck implies change, and most people are not willing to make the changes necessary in their lives to take advantage of the opportunities presented to them. Some people are lucky, but they make their own luck. They do that by their willingness to make necessary changes.

During the next 15 years, I worked for four different real estate and title companies and discovered that they all had one thing in common: lack of imagination and creativity. I tend to think outside the box, and this tendency of mine rattled my superiors, even though they benefited from the results of my efforts. When trying to inject some creativity into the business I not only met with opposition, but, in one case, a cease-and-desist order.

For one company I came up with an ad campaign titled "Be a Selfish Parent." To me this was a no-brainer in getting across the concept that this particular residential community was for adults. Children were certainly allowed to live there, but the condos and surroundings were set up for those grown-ups who had put in their time as parents and thought now was the time to do for themselves. The owners of the company received numerous phone calls from people saying they objected to the "anti-family" tone of the ad.

They believed that the ad implied that if you lived there, you were indeed selfish for thinking more of yourself than your kids.

These complainers were not far off the mark. But was it a good ad? You bet. Controversial, yes. But it got noticed and sold houses. Believe it or not, the president of the building company stopped running the ad. Why? He lived in the community and feared reprisals by his neighbors. I guess the message hit too close to home.

As for the cease-and-desist order, we come to an ad campaign I developed when I was director of sales and marketing for a building company. The ad's headline read: "Meet a Few of Our Best Architects." This ad featured prominent south Jersey men and women in front of the homes this builder had built for them.

The copy talked about how these people helped design their own homes, which was true in the sense that they worked with the architects and made recommendations for certain features that were included. Little did I know that the word "design" belonged to the Board of Architects in the state of New Jersey. I was suddenly in hot water. The Board of Architects said we were falsely portraying the people in the ads as professional architects. How ridiculous!

Did I give up on this ad? Nope. I went to one of my local elected officials and explained the absurdity of the situation. With his help, and my testimony in Trenton before a Senate subcommittee, this law was changed within nine months. The word "design" was free again!

I endured in this business much longer than I'd stayed anywhere else. I started at a real estate office in south Jersey, where I launched an ad campaign that proved to be very successful in moving high-end residential properties at a time when the real estate market was soft. This was my first—not to be my last—foray into sales, and I was quite good at it. I developed a sell piece that launched the concept of a Classic Homes Division for this particular company. Are you ever really impressed by those one-inch-by-one-inch photographs in real estate brochures that try to convey the grandeur of an expensive home? Neither am I. That's why I developed an entire brochure with large photos and not much type. No one before had produced such an elaborate sales piece to sell real estate. It was as inviting as the homes it advertised. And those properties moved—beyond our wildest expectations!

My efforts for this company were noticed, and I was

hired away by a title insurance company. This job turned out to be truly life changing, for it is there that I not only created innovative procedures for handling the refinancing of properties, and developed software to handle certain aspects of the business (remember, I majored in computers at college), but it is there that I met my second wife. That's a cute story, but more on that later.

This particular title insurance company had a problem and that problem, as I have mentioned, was refinancing. When you buy a house the first time, you've got a real estate agent who makes sure that everything goes smoothly with your mortgage, because otherwise the agent doesn't get his or her commission. But when you already own the house and want to refinance your mortgage, you're out there all by yourself. I created a form on the computer that tells the owner exactly what he has to do in order to refinance, namely, (1) termite certification, (2) appraisal, and (3) title report. This form authorized the title company I worked for to do these things for the owner and charge back the costs at the settlement. This form is now standard operating procedure for refinancing in New Jersey, but 13 years ago, no one had ever thought of it.

Now, the lesson here is that if I had thought when first offered this job that I'd never done anything like it before and probably couldn't do it, then I would have failed at it and it would not have worked out. But I didn't think that way, and my thinking out of the box has always helped me be successful in anything I've undertaken, whether in the very business side of life or the very personal.

I also developed for this title company a software program we called Sophie, which stands for Software Offering Personal Help in Escrows. It was a program that helped the company manage multiple escrow accounts and search back titles. It is still in use today.

My greatest accomplishment, though, was spotting a particularly good looking woman who worked at this company and having the nerve to talk to her. Remember, I was not a particularly bad looking fellow, but there was a lot of me and, because of certain frustrations I was experiencing in my work and the fact that I had an unsuccessful first marriage and was only recently divorced, my waistline was not getting any smaller.

But luck and timing were on my side! What happened was this! My office overlooked the parking lot and every day I would see this very attractive woman get out of her car and, at the end of the day, get back into it. Not only was I impressed with her, but I was impressed with her car. It was a really cool car for the time (this was 13 years ago)—a Datsun 240Z—and I noticed that she always kept the car very clean. Unbeknownst to me, this attractive woman's office was one floor above mine, and someone else in the office was trying to fix us up. But the right opportunity hadn't yet presented itself.

Now, the people who worked in this particular community always hung out at a certain bar/restaurant/nightclub and they naturally divided themselves up into two distinct groups: the after-work crowd, who headed to the establishment right after work, and the dressed-to-kill crowd, who went home right after work, and changed clothes before going out. I was part of the former group; this attractive woman was part of the latter, so our paths never crossed. One evening right after work, I was supposed to meet two buddies for a drink, but they never showed up. While I was waiting, this attractive woman—now dressed to kill—

walked in and it soon became apparent to me that whoever she was supposed to meet never showed up, either. I know it's a corny line, but as we were both waiting there, I said to her, "Don't I know you from somewhere?" Well, we started talking and we have never stopped. We were married one year later.

My innovative efforts at the title insurance company did not go unnoticed. A colleague who owned his own building company, Stein Built Homes, called me one day and told me he had a problem. Business was very good, but he was getting a lot of flak because he was falling behind in servicing customer complaints about his buildings. He asked me if I could dream up a service program that would satisfy his customers?

My immediate response: Sure, I can do that! I was eager to get out of the title business, but in all honesty, I didn't have the foggiest idea how to do what this fellow was asking of me. BUT, I was good at organization and I have a sense of humor, and I just jumped in. How complicated could it be, I wondered?

We can all take a lesson from this seemingly impulsive behavior. I learned this lesson when I was asked to take a test drive of a BMW. This was no ordinary test drive. This test was performed on a special course that was sprayed with water and soap to mimic a rain-slicked highway. We were instructed to drive along at 40 miles per hour and then slam on the brakes while doing a J-turn, the sharpest turn you can make in a car. The object was to avoid hitting any of the plastic orange cones that line the course. We were told that in order to avoid the cones, we had to keep our eyes fixed on where we wanted to end up, NOT on where the car was actually going at the moment. Now these instructions are a lot harder to follow than they appear. The class learned that it's a driver's instinct to look at where the car is actually headed, not where you want it to go. The first time through the course, every driver crashed through the cones, but the next time, when the instructions were repeated to stay fixed on the goal, we all maneuvered quite safely through the course. The point I took with me from this exercise is that whenever you are faced with a new challenge, it's imperative to keep the goal in clear view and head for it. If you keep your eye on where you think you are going or, worse yet, only on where you've been, you'll never reach the new goal. If I'd thought—Well, gee, I've never really done any job like that before, so how can I promise to do it now?—I would have never gotten the opportunity to test my wings and find out what I'm capable of.

What I devised for Mr. Stein—and it's become industry standard—is a paper system of filing the complaints. A complaint comes in and, instead of logging it into a computer file where no one would ever see it, it's put on a slip of paper and filed under the specific name of the builder. The builder comes into the office and if he'd got a stack of these complaint sheets, he knows he's got to not only make the repairs, but also make sure his workmanship improves so that these kinds of complaints don't get written up and filed in the first place. If the complaints were sitting in an electronic file somewhere, no one would ever see them or be able to judge the skill of the builder.

So I designed the form and then designed some policies for dealing with complaints. One policy was that every customer who calls gets a return phone call THAT DAY, no matter how late the builder has to stay to return all the phone calls.

It became apparent that we needed to keep our service vehicles clean and organized, so I devised a system in which every week when the service guy picks up his paycheck we would inspect his vehicle. The driver of the best-organized, best-maintained, and cleanest truck got a bonus in cash! You might have thought that the builders would object, but the guys really got into it, down to the last detail. One guy devised a way of organizing screws with a cup system and each screw taped to the top of the cup for easy identification.

This building company was having a problem with their walk-throughs. If you've ever bought a house or an apartment, you know about walk-throughs. It's that time scheduled a day or so before the closing when the real estate agent and the buyer literally "walk through" the property and note anything and everything that isn't in perfect shape and that must be fixed before the closing. This company was having problems because their builders were leaving way too many details to the last minute, which would either force a delay in the closing or drive the builder crazy with the pressure to complete the job on deadline.

Why is this so hard? If you went to a store and came home with a toaster that had 10 Post-it Notes on it about repairs the toaster needed before you could use it, would you find that acceptable? Of course not! Chances are great you'd never purchase the toaster in the first place. So when you walk into a closing is it acceptable to have a list of things that still need to be taken care of in the home you are purchasing?

I thought about a way of eliminating the long lists of things that had to be taken care of before the closing. I devised a checklist that contained a maximum of ten items that needed to be fixed in a property before it was ready for that first-time sale. If the house had 11 things that needed to be fixed, it wasn't ready for sale and the builder couldn't recoup his monetary layout. The system worked wonders, with houses coming to sale in much better shape than before I started. If the customer found more than ten things wrong in the house, the building company would fix them and charge costs back to the construction department. This procedure produced accountability and better quality, better built houses.

I made one more career move in the real estate industry before I left it, and that was to the firm of Pond & Spitz in south Jersey. I was head of marketing there, and I also trained the sales staff. I came up with a terrific idea for a brochure with the tagline "It's Included." that served as a guide to potential buyers in comparing what P&S's properties offered when compared to those of other real estate firms in the area. The four-page brochure offered an elaborate checklist of features ("upgraded kitchen cabinetry," "GE white-on-white kitchen appliances," "double self-cleaning ovens w/ separate microwave") and a list of the benefits of those features ("Our kitchen standards cost thousands more than other builders offer, plus offer higher resale value," "GE upgraded appliances offer you a name you can trust," " You can be cooking in two ovens at once, plus still use the microwave"). At the bottom of the brochure, the tagline summed it up: "A $60,000 difference you should check out before you buy!" What home buyer could resist this piece, which laid out all the benefits of buying condos from P&S?

This particular ad campaign was covered in the Philadelphia *Inquirer* (giving us the kind of attention that money simply can't buy), and it was a big hit. I was also able to save the firm lots of money by producing the master layout, which is quite complicated, at home using a very early version of a desktop publishing program that was just being released. As I mentioned, give me an instruction booklet and I can do anything. This desktop publishing program was, for me, a piece of cake and lots of fun, too; and the firm did not have to hire an outside public relations firm to produce it, as they'd done in the past.

I was rewarded for my efforts in every way except that there was no big "payoff." I was a salaried employee, yes, and I enjoyed the prestige of being elected president of the Builders League of South Jersey. P&S couldn't create big, fancy titles fast enough for me. I won the Realtor Association Award of the Year, and then went on to win the Marketing Director of the Year award by the National Association of Builders, which is quite an honor.

Meanwhile, my waistline was continuing to expand! Like many people, I was using food as a way to deal with stress. There were a variety of stress factors going through the residential real estate business in the Northeast through the late 1980s and early 1990s.

Business was down, and the downturn in housing cast a gloom over the company I was working for. Cuts in personnel were being called for, along with pay adjustments. Although I was as successful as possible, given the difficult conditions, the owners of the company looked to me to take a pay cut.

As for having a big title, it was my experience in real estate that the bigger the title, the smaller the paycheck. So I was given dual titles that came along with no increase in pay. One day I was called in and told, "You're doing a great job. We're going to promote you to general manager." This, while I was still director of marketing.

"With this new title," I asked, "what pay increase can I expect?"

Zip! was the answer.

So much for big titles.

So even though there were some high points in my real estate career, generally I remained unhappy and unfulfilled. Although the money wasn't terrific, the biggest problem was that my creative self was underutilized; I rarely got the chance to exercise my creative ability, which I viewed as my greatest strength (that, and my perseverance!). There were other frustrations I had, not so much with this firm, but with the real estate industry in general and its lack of planning for the future. So, there I was, in a troubled industry, with a big title on my business card, a small bank account, and an expanding waistline!

The end of my real estate career came when the firm I was with was about to be acquired by another firm, which would have been a good deal for all concerned. But, for reasons unknown to me, the deal fell through and soon after I found myself out of a job. It was a mutual parting of the ways, and one that might have devastated me had it not been for the fact that I was already looking ahead to the next phase of my life.

How I made the transition out of a "successful" 15-year-career in real estate to this new medium of electronic sales is an example of an opportunity presenting itself (luck) that I was prepared to act on (timing) and make the adjustments necessary to change my life.

Chapter Four

Transitions:
From Real Estate to Lite Bites®
in Several Easy Lessons

L ife is a series of transitions. Some you create and some come at you unexpectedly. The one constant in life is change, some of it good, some of it bad; you either roll with it or let it roll over you.

If you let the unexpected defeat you, well then, you're defeated. But if you take a positive approach, then you can't be beat.

After 15-plus years in real estate, one day I found myself out of a job—out of a job and out of a career. While in real estate, I had worked for at least three different companies, but with each change, the move was upward. But that didn't matter: I both quit and was fired at the same time, but in any case, I was out!

Frankly, I didn't want to get back in. I had done well in real estate, but my biggest disappointment was that the industry didn't prove to be a business where my brand of creativity was valued as highly as I thought it should be. True, I was working in it at a time when the market was depressed, so that probably made my employers less willing to take chances and spend money on the kinds of promotions I recommended and the kind of marketing approach I thought would enhance any business. Still, that career gave me experience that would become very useful to me. It had its high points and its low points, the low points resulting from frustrations brought on by lack of satisfaction, reward, and encouragement, which I gradually began to recognize were essential for my own well-being.

As for the high points, my weight ballooned—no doubt because of the stress and dissatisfaction—to well over 320 pounds.

It was sometime during my tenure at Pond & Spitz that Dad came back from that spa in Hawaii and handed me the Lite Bites® wafers. As I related earlier in this book, I tried them and lost 12 pounds without changing anything else in my life. I was intrigued that this change came about with no effort on my part, and I was greatly encouraged that there was something more to these wafers than was first apparent.

By now you know a bit about me and you know that whenever I do something, I do it whole hog. So when I finished all the wafers Dad had brought back from the spa, I didn't just reorder them over the phone or fax machine, I actually called up the manufacturers and began talking with them.

The manufacturers turned out to be none other than Cheryl and Dean Radetsky on the West Coast. Cheryl and Dean were passionate about changing the way people lose weight. They talked about empowerment and self-esteem. Instead of starvation and punishment, they talked about becoming a conscious eater and loving the body you were born with. But I was most impressed when they talked to me about their products as lovingly as most parents talk about their children. I was curious to know what the magic in Lite Bites was, and, if not magic, then what made the product work so well.

They told me: a custom herbal blend. While most power or diet bars contain no more than one or two herbs and lots of sugar, the Lite Bites custom herbal blend contains eight different herbs and other nutrients working together. The creators of Lite Bites carefully considered how these herbs work and how they synergistically affect the body. Cheryl and Dean could talk for hours on this subject, and what they had to say really fascinated me. In the next chapter, I go into more detail about each individual herb and what benefits we may gain by eating them in Lite Bites products. I also want to stress that the products work much more efficiently when used as part of the Lite Bites Fat-Fighting System, a four-step program involving planning, food, fitness, and attitude that is essential to a healthier lifestyle. The Lite Bites Fat-Fighting System is outlined in detail in chapters 5 and 6.

What I learned from the Radetskys in that initial conversation was this: one of the key ingredients in Lite Bites products has been studied for its ability to help inhibit the body's ability to convert excess calories into fat. It's that simple.

As to what happens to those calories and carbohydrates that aren't stored as fat, the body converts some of them to glycogen. Glycogen is energy for the body and the "I'm full" signal that your liver sends to your brain that tells you to stop eating. That's why, for the first time in my life, I was pushing food away.

I found out that if you eat one Lite Bites wafer an hour before a meal, your body starts working with you rather than against you toward your weight-loss goals. Although you can eat up to four wafers a day, I found that this very minimal change in my diet was having a major effect on my metabolism.

I also found out that other herbs and nutrients in Lite Bites have traditionally been used to aid in digestive regularity and help protect the liver against toxins and various disorders. Why is the liver so important? The liver is the fat-metabolizing organ in the body. Therefore, if you make the liver more efficient, it should metabolize more fat. Pretty cool, eh? Other ingredients do other things: help balance blood sugar levels, play an important role in sugar and fat metabolism, provide concentrated sources of energy, contain amino acids that help the body preserve lean muscle, and deliver vitamins that are required for the proper functioning of the body . . . and much more. All these ingredients act together to support the body in feeling satisfied and providing important nutrition for weight management. But the best part about the bars is that they simply taste delicious. And they work! Ask anyone who's tried one.

I was tremendously excited about what I was hearing. I had been on so many diets in my life that I had dieted my way up to over 320 pounds. (That's when I stopped weighing myself.) And, as I heard the Radetskys talk, I realized that I had not failed on those diets. The diets had failed me. Here were the Radetskys, offering me an alternative to the yo-yo weight-loss programs I had encountered my entire life. Perhaps Dad was right: If these wafers continued to work for me, then I would have a good story to share on the air with QVC viewers.

I was ready for a change and when that change came, I realized that all the selling, all the marketing, all the innovations I tried to do in my marketing job in real estate paid off. I had learned the difference between features and benefits to the customers of Pond & Spitz houses, and that concept would serve me well as I thought about how to present

Lite Bites on the air. My next venture would use all the talents, all the experience, and all the wisdom I'd managed to gather in my working and creative life—and at last, the monetary rewards would come. But I realized that that was not the most important reward. What was? In short, how I look and feel about myself and who I am. Those rewards are, as the ads now say, priceless!

Here's what happened.

I continued to consume Lite Bites wafers—the frosted bars in different flavors had not yet been developed—and I continued to lose weight. I also continued my discussions with the Radetskys about the benefits of the product and the right way (slow and easy) to lose weight. At the same time, I began efforts to get the producers at QVC to consider scheduling a spot. My dad had, by this time, "retired" from QVC—it was the twentieth company he had founded and within a few years had turned over to others—but fortunately, Mike Boyd, the executive who'd asked me to leave the Franklin Mint after I'd asked for that raise, was also a past president of QVC and was to become one of my biggest supporters. In fact, Mike became the mentor we all need when we're making a career switch. If you need any evidence of how it's never a good idea to burn bridges in your career or in your life, this is it! Mike helped me not only position Lite Bites, but had also got my first venture into product marketing on the air, even before I'd ever encountered Lite Bites. While I was still working in real estate, I turned to him with this crazy idea I had.

Golf had never been a big area for QVC. But I loved golf and felt that QVC viewers would buy golf products if they were simply offered them. I called Edwin Watts, who is one of the biggest retailers of golf sporting equipment in

Florida, out of the blue one day and worked very hard to convince him that he ought to appear on QVC with his golf equipment. I developed a pitch that I thought would appeal to the viewers. The show aired in June 1995. This show was a big risk because at that time I had no idea what I was doing. I didn't appear on this segment; Edwin did the on-air segment himself. It was not as successful as it could have been, but I now know in hindsight what we did wrong: We gave the viewer too many choices. One thing I've learned about being on QVC: KEEP IT SIMPLE. Don't give the viewer too many choices in a limited amount of airtime. Instead of giving the viewer a choice of two or three drivers and three different shafts, as we did, we should have showed one club and said, "This 12-degree lofted driver with regular gear shaft is just right for the average golfer, and here's why." Then we could have listed ten benefits of this particular club. Because I advised Edwin to present as much product as possible, the viewers got confused and didn't know what the heck to order. I learned a lot from the results of this show.

At the time I developed the golf club offering, I was still working in real estate and exploring some entrepreneurial marketing opportunities for QVC. With Lite Bites, I thought I had a product that just might work. I had tried them, I thought they were great, I had a story to tell about them, and I also happened to be the son of QVC's founder, so credibility with the audience could be established.

I began to develop my presentation to the buyer, the first step in the long road to get products on the air at QVC. More about that in upcoming chapters. All I'll say here is that, when I did make my presentation, it just didn't fly. I approached the Health and Fitness buyer with all my facts and all my enthusiasm, only to be turned down because this particular department wasn't doing ingestible diet products at that time. See, in the end, it really makes no difference whether you're the boss's son or not. It may help get you through the door, but from then on, you're just like everyone else. Several months later, I started all over again. But this time I got an appointment to present Lite Bites to the Health and Beauty buyer, who accepted the product and thought I should be the product's spokesperson. I was on my way!

It was at this point that I lost my job in real estate! Talk about timing! Here I was, out of a job and out of a career. After losing my real estate job, I felt hurt and betrayed. After all, I had devoted a decade and a half of my life to this business, and in one day, I was out. I disagreed with some coworkers about where the business was going. I wanted definite answers about where we were headed, and there were none. I could have just stayed on and coasted, but in life, as in flying, I like to know where I'm going.

Let me tell you, that was a tough moment. Where do I go, what do I do? I was left without a life raft.

I already knew what I was going to be doing next—the live Lite Bites spot had been scheduled but it was 12 weeks away—and I had no idea how successful that venture might be. That spot amounted to one ten-minute presentation that would either turn into a bust or become a hit. There would likely be no in-between.

Here was the quandary. I'd been in the real estate business most of my professional life, was scared of public speaking, and now was going on-air into 60 million homes all across America. Talk about change, and talk about the uncertainty of your future!

What made me all the more anxious was that while I was in that three-month waiting period before going on QVC, I was offered a job in the building business with a salary upwards of $75,000-a-year, and I turned it down.

Is that crazy, or does it reflect a strong belief in myself and Lite Bites, the product I was preparing to introduce on national TV?

I knew this much, though. I believed in the product, I knew it worked, and I was willing to stake my future on it. But it was not an easy decision to make. At that time in my life, it was not easy to turn down a $75,000 a year job.

But life is full of such crossroads, and there comes that moment when you have to decide which road to take. Once you've made the decision to change, you have to move forward. As a friend reminded me, if you look backwards, the only thing you get is a stiff neck. You only see where you've been and not where you're going.

So in those three crucial months between jobs, I spent a lot of the time preparing for the new challenge.

For a time I was scared to death, but soon enough, I was committed to the change. My attitude was to be positive and optimistic. Okay, I did not know ahead of time that I would do well with Lite Bites, but I was confident in my abilities.

The crux of it is that if you believe you're going to fail, you're going to fail. I learned that lesson in a driving school of high performance BMWs that I talked about in the previous chapter, where you are taught that if you make an emergency breaking maneuver at high speeds while having to turn and look where you think you're going to go instead of where you want to go, you're going to crash. The first time I tried to brake in that emergency maneuver, I had an accident.

But, in this class, when we were all told to look where we

wanted to go, instead of where we thought we were going to go, we all executed the maneuver perfectly the second time through.

This lesson applies to more than just operating a high-speed automobile. It applies to all of life. Expect to fail and you will fail. Expect to succeed and you are far less likely to crash.

I guess that's the approach I took when finding myself between careers.

I steered myself directly in the direction I wanted to go.

I stayed focused and kept my eyes on the ball, to use a phrase common among pilots.

Eventually, by staying the course, three things happened. I began with an expanding waistline, a decreasing bank account, and a big title on my business card. I turned it all around through QVC and Lite Bites.

After Lite Bites was accepted by the QVC buyer, the first step was a spot on Q2, a smaller sister network with studios just outside of New York City. This spot would serve as a kind of testing ground both for me and for the product. If I did well, then I'd probably have a shot at a spot on QVC, which reached out to more than ten times the audience of Q2. If I didn't . . .

I prepared for this spot for months. I listed features and benefits, got my own experience with Lite Bites down pat. I rehearsed using flash cards that contained my ten main points. It was quite an intense period of my life.

I had practiced the details of my own personal weight struggles, how I had been introduced to the bars, all the benefits that using Lite Bites provided. Now, I do credit my father with that stick-to-it-ness that dictates when you make a commitment, you stick with it, see it through to completion, and

give it your all. I also credit my father with my tendency to
overtrain, overprepare, be ready for any eventuality in anything I do. You've read in these pages how I don't ever do
anything halfway. I'm careful not to spread myself too thin,
because I don't want to disappoint anyone. To this day, I am
well organized, and that sense of organization and commitment to carry through to the goal line came from him.

But one week before my scheduled appearance, with my
nerves frayed and my mind focused on that one appearance
only, Dad threw me a curve ball. I received a package from
him that contained a stack of memos he had written when
he was running QVC, and a note that read, "Call me. Dad."
The memos were from him to his producers, vice presi-
dents, and others, and they pointed out everything the on-air
hosts had done WRONG during their spots. This was his
way of reaching out to help me as I prepared to take the
biggest career risk of my life, but the contents of these
memos unnerved me.

Some of the items were routine grousings:
- Don't unnecessarily touch smudgeable parts of products.
- Don't wear clothes that are so loud as to be distracting, and
  don't wear solid white outfits, which cause the camera lens
  to close down and make the show host's face too dark.
- Please avoid using the word "sold" when you mean to
  say "ordered."

But some of his points involved legal issues or credibility
issues, such as:
- The word "never" should not be used. It's a dangerous
  word that can only get us in trouble. Expunge it from
  our vocabulary.

- "One Time" means one time. If we offer the item a second time at that special price, even during the same hour, it can damage our credibility . . .
- Please remind the show hosts to avoid making a fuss about the location of callers who live near us . . . I realize that such statements are a natural conversation response, but that kind of response must be avoided because it is counterproductive . . . It also tends to remind viewers on the West Coast how far away they are . . .
- There is a correct way and an incorrect way to present the 30-day money back guarantee. The correct way is to emphasize the fact that we guarantee satisfaction. We do that by means of our 30-day money back guarantee. The incorrect way is to suggest that any item should be ordered just to try it out . . . .

The items in these memos went on and on for what seemed like forever. Here I was, nervous about my first appearance on television, sweating, and upset before I received these salvos from Dad, and now I had to worry about every syllable that would come out of my mouth.

Imagine the pressure!

On my trip up to New York, I kept reviewing the different herbs and nutrients contained in the Lite Bites products. My main concern was to be factual without being overly complex and technical about the benefits to viewers of the ingredients found in the bars.

I arrived at Q2's studio early on the morning of January 11, 1996. I was a bundle of nerves, and energy. Before I knew what was happening, I was getting makeup—for the first time in my life, of course.

I rallied myself, focused on what I wanted to say about Lite Bites. At 8 A.M., I appeared with my first station host of the day, went on the air before the cameras and millions of viewers, told my story of being the founder's son and finding this product that caused me to lose weight almost effortlessly, and—before I knew it—the spot was over!

Since the Lite Bites wafers were what was called the "Resolution Item of the Day," I appeared seven more times in the next ten hours, each time with a different host. I got more on-air experience in that one day than most guests get in an entire year.

But the best news was that the wafers were the top selling item of the day and sold out completely by day's end.

After the show, Dad called me up and gave me notes on my performance. You have to remember that this is a man who was quite used to running the whole show. While he was still in charge at QVC, I remember we'd be having a family dinner with the TV turned on in the background, tuned to QVC, of course. No matter what course was being served, he would sometimes stop, pick up the phone, and dial in straight to the director and suggest to him a change in the camera angle, or another tact to take than the one that was being taken at the moment—on-air! So I expected his comments after my first appearance. He was trying to be helpful—his attention to details is a trait that many successful entrepreneurs share and is what has made QVC great. He was impressed with my knowledge of the product, but commented that I spoke more about features of the product than about benefits to the customer. He felt my presentation was too scientific, that I used too many terms that didn't trip off the tongue easily and convincingly. There is a difference, he explained, between being specific and overly technical.

He said I went into too much detail about my personal story, too much detail about how exactly the herbs worked. At this point, I politely interrupted him. Dad, I explained, I'm enthused about Lite Bites and what it did for me and I thought I conveyed that enthusiasm well. I'm sure I did something right!

Neither one of us was right or wrong! However valid his points were, the product sold out by the end of the day. I did incorporate most of his suggestions later on, but at the moment, I was relieved the appearance was over and seemed to have been a success.

The next step was to convince the buyer to accept the product for an on-air segment on QVC; that was the big one where I needed to land a "hole-in-one." That finally happened eight months after the product was initially accepted by the QVC Health and Beauty buyer; three months after my successful Q2 appearance. That period was, for me, a period of planning, preparing, talking with other Lite Bites enthusiasts, and working, with the Radetskys, while they developed the Lite Bites Fat-Fighting System, which is so important to weight loss success. It's not enough to eat the Lite Bites Fat-Fighting System's wafers or bars; as we'll discuss in a later chapter, the products are only part of a complete lifestyle change. While at my highest weight I was reluctant to begin an exercise program, now, at that weight minus 30 pounds, I was able, with my doctor's guidance, to begin a fitness program that was not only good for me, but made me feel like a million bucks. Today, I exercise regularly and actually look forward to those hours I put in, whether on the golf course, or skiing, or horseback riding.

The big day finally came. My first appearance on QVC! I took my father's advice and had planned to simplify the benefits of the Lite Bites products. On-air, before millions of viewers, I explained the Lite Bites Fat-Fighting System, and of course told my personal story of being the founder's son and finding this product that caused me to lose weight almost effortlessly. Having then talked about a few of the bars' benefits, I remember looking at a clock at about four minutes and thinking, oh, no, I will run out of things to say before my ten-minute time slot is up! And then, all of a sudden, at four and a half minutes, the product sold out! And I was off the air before getting to the remaining benefits of the product! Apparently viewers responded to the fact that I was the founder's son and expressed their trust in QVC. If the founder's son said it was a good product, that was really all the viewers who wanted a lifestyle change needed to hear.

I found out later something quite poignant about that first appearance: My father was waiting on the phone line to be cued in to talk to me—on-air, before millions of viewers!—to congratulate me on my first QVC appearance. But the product sold out so quickly that there was no time to take his call. How I would have loved to have received that call at just that moment!

Although it wasn't immediately apparent, I was well on my way to another career and a very satisfying and highly creative one, that of being "the Lite Bites man" and of expanding into product positioning for other QVC hopefuls. Today, my waistline is slimmer, my bank account somewhat fatter, and I have NO title on my business card. I accept new clients only by referral. And it all happened because of luck, timing and life. I was presented with a product, those first Lite Bites wafers, at a time in my life when I needed a change, and I was open enough to the product and the process to accept the changes that I had to make in order to make my life a success—on my own terms. I am not saying that making those changes from real estate to product positioning was easy—not at all. In fact, it was very stressful! But I stuck to it and the rewards have been substantial.

My point in revealing all these details about my life is to show you that I was just a middle-aged guy with a weight problem, a career problem, and the low self-esteem that goes along with all that, and with a little luck, at the right time, I turned my life around. And you can, too.

—

Here are the parting words of a speech I made when I stepped down as the president of the Builders League of South Jersey: "In addition to the many things I learned about business, I need to thank this industry for one other thing: my weight gain. Because without that I would not have had my next success. Which was my weight loss, and my chance to tell my story on QVC."

I made that speech after I had been at QVC for more than a year. I served out my term as president of this prestigious organization because I was on the executive ladder and felt an obligation to the industry. Though I did not have all the satisfaction I wanted in this business, it's where I made many friends, some of whom I still do business with. Even today, as far away from the industry as I am, I will serve as chairman for a benefit or industry fundraiser. I still have friends in the industry, including the Pond & Spitz folks who had been my last employers. I'm a loyal guy, and it's always a good idea to keep those contacts flowing and not to burn bridges.

Before ending this chapter, let me touch again on dealing with failure, or as I'd rather put it, perceived failure. Focus on the things you did accomplish and are capable of accomplishing again.

First on the agenda—keep busy. While I was in transition, I prepared myself personally and professionally. I made some improvements to our home, and even managed a political campaign. Those initial three months just flew by.

In other words, don't let yourself stagnate. Be ready for the next big opportunity. Where will that opportunity come from? From your network of family, friends, and colleagues.

In the next chapters, I'll get more specific about the properties and the benefits of the Lite Bites Fat-Fighting System and share with you the stories of some real-life folks who found success—as *they* define it—using the Lite Bites products.

Part Two
The Lite Bites®
Fat-Fighting System

Chapter Five

Lite Bites® to the Rescue

This section of the book is one of my favorites, because I'm not only going to go into more detail about my own success story using Lite Bites products, but I'm going to share with you some of the comments I've received from others who have been equally successful with the Lite Bites Fat-Fighting System. My goal in this chapter is merely to tell more about HOW it works. You'll hear stories from others who have been successful in losing weight with Lite Bites—and I hope this will begin to motivate you to make lifestyle changes on your own. Later, I will outline in detail a program you can follow to start your own healthy lifestyle routine using the Lite Bites Fat-Fighting System.

One note: the statements from other Lite Bites users you'll read throughout this chapter are true. I've gathered them from REAL people who I've met either on the air or through letters and phone calls we've exchanged. But for those who have not appeared on-air, I've given you only their first names and a general area of residence.

From my experience, I think you have a better chance of being struck by lightning than losing weight from a commercial weight-loss program. Those of you who've gone through what I did know exactly what I'm talking about—false hopes, unrealistic goals, and weight-loss programs that are temporary. You need a permanent lifestyle change for permanent weight loss.

Since I began shedding pounds and became a fixture on QVC by championing Lite Bites, I have repeatedly been asked two questions. First, how did I lose the weight; second, how did I put on so much weight?

Let's tackle the second question first.

As I like to say, I dieted my way to over three hundred pounds. I did that because like most people in this country—and let's remember that more than half of all Americans are overweight—I wanted instant gratification. Instant results.

In this country we're always in a hurry, always out for the shortcut, and if you'll pardon me for a philosophical moment, that drive is what has made us great; but it has also made us fat. The same impatience that leads us to a lust for food also prompts us to search for quick, easy diets.

So we tend to overdiet, and that's the crux of the problem.

Most experts will tell you, and I could not agree more, that you should not lose more than four to six pounds per month. What we forget is that we did not put on the weight quickly; therefore, we should not take it off quickly.

What happens when you diet too quickly? Not to get too technical, but it's important to know some elementary facts about our bodies. When weight starts going down fast, your body's genetic code thinks you're some sort of caveman walking across a desert looking for the next oasis and the next meal. What is actually happening is that your metabolism rate—the rate at which the body burns calories—actually goes down, and you begin to store fat. Instead of losing body fat, you are storing more body fat.

So when you overdiet your body actually preserves fat as long as possible and starts breaking down muscle to get the energy it needs.

That's just the opposite of what you want.

Then it only gets worse. When you eventually do eat, your body takes some of those calories and carbohydrates and stores them as more fat—because it wants to prepare itself for its next starvation period.

In my case—and in the case of so many other Americans —I entered a number of commercial weight-loss programs when I felt it was time to get myself fit and in shape. As one viewer (Dr. Lucky from Long Island, New York, a middle-aged woman with a degree in forensic pathology who lost over 130 pounds) told me, "When I finally got to the point in my life where I wanted to lose weight, I tried EVERY-THING. Lite Bites was the only program that worked."

Many of you have probably had that experience. I certainly did. I won't name names, but the programs I enrolled in, well, they're the ones that require you to bring your own meals with you. How practical is that for preparing you for how you really should be eating?

From what I understand, there is a 90% failure rate from commercial weight-loss programs. The fact is, you have to change your lifestyle in order to lose weight and keep it off. The problem with diets is that eventually you stop dieting. In many cases, diets damage your metabolism and promote future fat storage. Some are just foolish, in my opinion.

For example, one so-called diet is a fat-burning soup diet. Puh-leeze! To me, this is so absurd. Not only does this system rely on the quick weight-loss approach, but you're expected to carry around containers of soup wherever you go.

The soup, by the way, has a broth made of onions, scallions, and pepper. If your body is anything like mine, you're bound to end up a very lonely person. Onions, no less! You'll have the worst gas imaginable and are likely to be thin but alone.

Getting back to the cause of weight gain: In my case I was conditioned to reward myself with food *and* to drown my sorrows in food.

Clothing is another trap. There are some nationally known fashion consultants who say, "Don't worry about the label size. Buy what fits." To which I say, "Uh-oh." Just like you tend to fill up everything on your computer hard drive no matter how great its capacity, so you will fill up your clothing, no matter what the size.

Speaking of clothing, one viewer sent me a letter with the word HELP! "I've been using Lite Bites products for eight weeks. I haven't lost any weight, but I've lost four and a half inches off my waist. What am I doing wrong?"

Here's what's "wrong." Absolutely nothing! The explanation is that muscle weighs more than fat. In this case, if your body is starting to recompose itself, you are probably building muscle and losing fat. So the scale weight may stay the same, but your clothes are starting to fit better—and you'll probably feel better, too!

That's why it's important to visit your doctor before you start any weight-loss program and have your body fat measured.

Another temptation we all face are these so-called fat-free products. People forget what I've been saying for years on QVC—fat free is not *body* fat free. We are eating more "fat-free" products than ever, and yet the typical American is ten pounds heavier than ever. The problem is obvious. We tend to eat more fat-free products, but excess calories, fat-free or not, still get converted into body fat.

I read in a recent magazine article about an experiment that proved that given a choice between one very rich cookie and a plate full of fat-free cookies, most people went to town on the fat-free cookies. These people didn't realize that they'd probably be consuming fewer calories if they ate only one very rich cookie.

That's the beauty of the Lite Bites Fat-Fighting System. If this sounds familiar to you, it's because Lite Bites changed my life. It has worked for me—I've lost 80 pounds of body fat—as well as for tens of thousands of QVC viewers. With Lite Bites, you eat what you want. You just tend to eat less. Plus, you feel full sooner. You start being the one in control.

All in all, though, it's not just your weight or your size that counts, it's how healthy you are. As I say on the air, "I want you to be healthy, not skinny." Here's what I mean by that. A recent article appeared about a certain triathlete (triathletes are characteristically thin) who weighed over 250 pounds. By all standards, he was healthier than many traditionally built triathletes. He had a better heart rate and triglyceride level than his colleagues. Simply put, the man was healthy, no matter what he weighed.

So that's the bottom line. You may be somewhat overweight, but if you're healthy it's okay.

Listen, if your goal in life is to look like an anorexic 14-year-old, you're probably going to fail. That fashion model look is not the way to go for most of us.

There is no magical product for weight loss. Most successful programs aren't programs at all, but merely you doing things on your own through your own initiative. This means that you have made choices that are right for you.

In short, you have a better chance of losing weight—and keeping it off—when you diet on your own. Now, about Lite Bites to the rescue. As I've mentioned, about two and a half years ago, my father introduced me to Lite Bites wafers. He came across the product while visiting a spa. I tasted the wafers and found them dry, which is actually a good thing because the dryness encouraged me to drink a lot of water. The product doesn't taste as good as the newer Lite Bites products, yet it is still a favorite among QVC viewers. Viewers tell me they have a wafer when they want a crunchy snack, but not necessarily something sweet.

Remember, like most dieters, I was able to successfully lose weight quickly, and was even more successful in putting the weight back on quickly. In most cases I put on more weight than I took off.

I started using the wafers. Like most dieters who've been through everything, I was skeptical. I didn't expect the wafers to do the trick. But the results were stunning!

Without counting a calorie or a carbohydrate, and without even trying to watch what I was eating, I lost almost 12 pounds in about six weeks.

Now I was motivated. I just lost 12 pounds without even trying, and I felt I could continue on with a new weight loss goal of 25 pounds. This is important because most people try to lose weight for the wrong reasons. It's usually for a major life event, such as a wedding, a new boyfriend or girlfriend, or a class reunion.

Unexpectedly, I was in control. With Lite Bites I was solely in command of my eating habits.

To see whether or not I was hallucinating, I got checked by a doctor, who confirmed the bad shape I'd been in for so long, and the distance I still had to go. I still weighed over 300 pounds, my triglycerides were 236 (the recommended limit is 150), my blood pressure was a whopping 132 over 90. Not the picture of health. But it was good to have the information for the sake of comparison at a later date.

I discussed Lite Bites with my doctor. He encouraged me to go on with the product, but questioned how it would work. Many doctors don't understand herbal-based products.

Essentially what he said was, 'Can't hurt.' Anything that would help me lose weight had to be a good thing. Looking back now at the success of Lite Bites, for myself and others, I do not find myself faulting the doctor's skepticism. Of course doctors know their stuff, but remember, in four years of medical school, a typical doctor gets two and a half hours of instruction in nutrition.

I continued using Lite Bites and started to lose even more weight. In addition, I started to exercise.

My first goal was to lose 25 pounds. Setting goals for yourself—achievable goals, step by step—is crucial. I have now lost 80 pounds of body fat over a period of two years. But if my purpose was to lose 80 pounds at the beginning, I never would have done it.

So it's wise to establish small, obtainable goals. Large ones can become discouraging.

Another key to success, in my case, is that I did not and do not deprive myself of special treats when appropriate. When you go to a restaurant known for its great steak or cheesecake, go for it! Just don't eat the whole cheesecake, and don't do it every day.

The point is, if you deprive yourself too much, you'll end up saying "the heck with it," and you'll tend to indulge and keep on indulging.

What's the magic in Lite Bites? Dr. Lucky calls them "little miracles in wrappers." Well, it's not magic but this is what makes it click—a custom herbal blend. While most energy bars contain no more than one or two herbs, the Lite Bites custom herbal blend contains 8 different herbs and nutrients working together with 22 vitamins and minerals. Cheryl and Dean Radetsky, the creators of Lite Bites, carefully considered how these ingredients work together and how they synergistically affect the body.

I remember my first face-to-face meeting with Cheryl after months of "meetings" on the phone. I wore my old fat suit that fit if I bunched up the back with a tight belt. (I had shrunk from size 56 to size 46.) Cheryl's background was in biochemistry and herbalism. Dean had been in the weight-loss management business. They were walking encyclopedias on weight management and natural medicine. After years of R & D, they launched an all-natural product that used herbs from all over the world. This product helped the body reduce its ability to convert excess calories into fat when used as part of the Lite Bites Fat-Fighting System.

I don't want to get too, too technical, but many viewers have wondered exactly what it is that makes the Lite Bites products so effective. There are several key ingredients, including chromium, an essential mineral known to help regulate blood sugar levels in the body. You know that afternoon energy dip when you want to reach for a candy bar to restore your energy level? What chromium does is even out the dip, so that it's less severe and helps you control those cravings. Your blood sugar level does not crash, and therefore you don't have those awful cravings.

Another key ingredient is Citrin®, an extract of garcinia cambogia. Garcinia cambogia is a citrus fruit that grows in

Thailand and India. It may sound exotic, but it's been studied for over 30 years for its ability to help inhibit the body's ability to convert excess calories into fat. This extract enables the body to produce more glycogen. The glycogen is a complex carbohydrate that signals the brain that the body has all the food it needs. You then eat less, and there are fewer calories available for the body to store as fat. Beautiful, eh?

A third key ingredient is L-Carnitine. It's an amino acid that helps the body build lean muscle mass. Many athletes take it to build muscle. As I've said, it's no secret that when you lose a lot of weight quickly, you are NOT burning off fat, you're eating up your muscle mass. This amino acid helps maintain lean muscle mass as the pounds slowly come off.

As for the special herb and nutrient blend, the information is fascinating. Here's what I found out about some of the ingredients contained in Lite Bites products:

- Dandelion root, which may aid in digestive regularity and may also help the liver. It's known to be a hardy herb and a safe one.
- Schizandra berries, which may protect the liver against toxins and various disorders.
- Dong quai, a traditional Chinese medicine that is taken as a blood tonic to invigorate circulation.
- Royal jelly, a highly concentrated source of energy.
- Gymnema sylvestre, an herb that is known to balance out blood sugars.
- Kola nut extract, which aids in fat being released from fat cells.
- Hawaiian spirulina, one of the most nutrient-rich foods in the world.

Cheryl and Dean explained to me that the bars also contain 22 vitamins and minerals. The synergy of these ingredients when combined with a specific nutritional profile (high in carbohydrates, low in fat) is what makes them special and what makes them work so well together. Many of you have read about the benefits of soy protein and oat bran. Long before those studies were generally known, the Radetskys had figured out the benefits of those ingredients and had added them to Lite Bites shakes.

One other point the Radetskys emphasized to me was the biochemistry of weight loss. The way they explained it is this: If the body is to use calories and carbs effectively, the body's interdependent systems have to be functioning efficiently. We all know—and, let's face it, probably envy— people who seem to be able to eat like horses and never gain an ounce. The reason is that their bodies are much better at disposing of excess calories than my body is, and yours. That means that their bodies don't allow excess calories to turn to fat. The Lite Bites products used in conjunction with the Lite Bites Fat-Fighting System can support the body's own natural ability to metabolize calories. Some Lite Bites users claim their metabolism is now like that of their thinnest friends. How do I know that? I was speaking recently with Lite Bites success story Julie Carson from Pennsylvania. She lost 45 pounds in six months using the Lite Bites Fat-Fighting System. She told me, "Marv! Guess what? Through the holidays, I have not gained one ounce!" Now you know and I know about the holidays, and I would imagine that Julie did a bit of indulging during that period of time. Since she did not gain an ounce, my hunch is that her metabolism is working a lot more efficiently now than it did before she began eating Lite Bites.

Cheryl and Dean explained to me how Lite Bites differed from other energy or diet bars. While other products may contain one or two of the herbs that are used in Lite Bites, Lite Bites uses a precise synergy of herbal ingredients, including the three key ingredients I mentioned earlier and the others that have been used to help digestion and the function of the liver.

Plus, often the first ingredient listed in those other bars is, you guessed it, sugar! So sure, they give you an energy boost, but does it last? Does it help your body metabolize fat? Does it increase the efficiency of energy production? Certainly not the way Lite Bites Fat-Fighting System products do. Look on any Lite Bites bar. What's the first ingredient? No-fat-added granola. Good stuff!

With the Lite Bites Fat-Fighting System, the average weight loss is four to six pounds per month. Every doctor I know has told me that that is the proper amount of weight to lose. When you lose weight more quickly than that, you don't reset the body's metabolic setpoint. I'm sure you've seen these ads in the back of magazines or on buses: Lose 30 pounds in 30 days. Bad idea, because your body can't readjust its metabolic setpoint in that short amount of time. Simply put, your body's tendency is to always go back to its previous weight. If you lose weight more slowly, the body has time to adjust. But if you lose weight TOO slowly, then you tend to get discouraged, particularly if you have a lot of weight to lose.

Some QVC viewers keep telling me that they have lost weight without even exercising. However, as we'll discuss in the next chapter, if you add a little exercise along with your Lite Bites, you'll add more muscle mass. An added pound of muscle burns 50 calories a day. The pound of fat it replaces only burned two calories a day. To me, exercise is a no-brain-er. Besides, you'll feel so much better than you do today if you make exercise a part of your Lite Bites routine.

The bottom line is this: With the Lite Bites Fat-Fighting System, you should finally feel in control and be able to lose weight while still feeling satisfied. In other words, you won't be hungry.

Julie, whom you met earlier, addresses this very point. Not only did she lose 45 pounds, but she also dropped three dress sizes, and lost seven inches off both her waist and her hips. She told me recently, "Lite Bites products really do curb my appetite. I am a chocoholic, so I'm not satisfied unless I have the taste of chocolate after a meal. I get the peanut butter fudge bars on autodelivery and also the choco-late caramel Chewies. They taste good—in fact, they taste so good I call them 'my license to cheat.' They also take a while to eat, and, with some water, I feel really satisfied. I've been on every diet there is, but Lite Bites is a lifestyle. I'll be 40 soon, and gravity is NOT in my favor! I've lost the weight gradually, with no wrinkles, no bags, no sags!"

Dr. Lucky, whom you met earlier in this chapter, makes a similar point when she talks about Lite Bites. She lost 130 pounds. The first 20 came off when she was on another weight-loss program. Those 20 pounds took eight months to come off and she got discouraged. Then she tried Lite Bites and today, another 110 pounds lighter, she calls them her "legalized cheating mechanism." Chocolate was NOT Dr. Lucky's problem—what she craved was Italian food. "Lite Bites stopped my cravings dead in their tracks. I have two Ph.D.'s, one in nuclear physics and one in forensic patholo-gy. Not only that, but I have four master's degrees and I'm a licensed psychologist. Obviously I buried myself in academia because there were certain problems in my life that I simply could not face. During that fat time in my life, I did not want to interact with people because early in my career, I was assaulted by one of my patients who unexpectedly went berserk. Let me just say that I'm lucky to be alive, but I then got big and fat so that kind of attack would never happen to me again. I went from 115 pounds to well over 200 pounds.

"Well, I finally turned my life around and then I moved on! Once I decided to lose the weight, I tried EVERYTHING, and the Lite Bites Fat-Fighting System is the ONLY thing that worked for me. Not only did I lose weight, but my skin is wonderful. I also have more energy."

After my first time on-air, I quickly discovered that the QVC viewer trusted me because I was the founder's son. This was obvious because we sold out in four and a half minutes before even mentioning the product or how it works.

Dr. Lucky told me, "Honestly, Marv, Lite Bites is fantastic, but for me, you are the key. We've never met but you have really been there for me. You've been very caring and responsive on the phone. You seem to me to be a modest man. I truly believe you are not out for stardom, that you are out there to help people because you've been through it yourself and you know what a struggle it is to lose a lot of weight."

Indeed I do. I include comments like that not to toot my own horn, but to reinforce a key element in the success of Lite Bites and of QVC: viewers trust us. They know all products are thoroughly tested before they are ever offered on the air. More about that in a later section of this book.

Back to my first on-air appearance: I was prepared with all the necessary information about Lite Bites, but that first-time experience posed a shocking reality to me. I was to become the fat-fighting guy at QVC. I knew being the founder's son was going to mean something to the QVC viewer, but I had no idea how much of an impact it was going to make.

QVC viewers trusted QVC. Therefore they trusted the founder's son. This was the payoff: for once, being the boss's son really worked for me and for Lite Bites. Viewers reasoned that if the founder's son lost weight with the product, they were going to try it even though they did not know precisely how it worked.

Kathy Fodge from East Prairie, Missouri, comments on just this point. Kathy is an amazing Lite Bites success story. She first appeared on-air with me on September 17, 1998, and appeared again on my first live-audience broadcast on January 10, 1999. Kathy, who weighed over 300 pounds before she started the Lite Bites Fat-Fighting System, has lost 150 pounds in two years. She went from a size 28 to size 8! In fact, the first time she ever flew on an airplane was to appear on QVC, because she could never fit into an airplane seat before she lost the weight with Lite Bites. She told me that she had seen me on QVC several times before she decided to order the product. "And every time you appeared," she said, "you had lost more weight and you looked great! I knew QVC and I knew that if the product didn't work for me, I could get my money back, so there was no risk. I had tried every weight-loss product in the book, and they'd work for a while and then they just didn't work any more. I knew I had to do something about my weight. I travel a lot for my job and didn't have any time or any interest in attending weekly support meetings. When I stopped attending the meetings, the weight would just come back on.

"The bars taste good! They're satisfying, filling. They curb my appetite, so I eat less. They are a healthy product—the label tells me that. My doctor says I'm in better health now than I have been in years. I'm now 46 years old and that's quite a statement!

"The great part about Lite Bites is that they now help me keep the weight off. I don't need to lose any more weight, so I now use them for maintenance, and they work just great! I would recommend this product to anyone who needs to lose weight—that's why I agreed to a return appearance on QVC. The product has my seal of approval, and I want everyone to know it."

I find it interesting that, more than two years after my first appearance on QVC, the viewers think of Lite Bites and Marvin Segel as being one and the same. I'm the Lite Bites man, but I want to assure you that I'm just a regular guy who, as Dr. Lucky says, has been there, done that; that is, lost a lot of weight and kept it off.

My preparation for that first appearance came to good use. I spent months studying how Lite Bites worked. Like a little kid, I kept asking Cheryl and Dean how this product worked—and I got the answers I needed.

When Dad said to me, "If these work for you, then you might want to share your story as a testimonial on TV," I never in my wildest dreams thought I would end up where I am today. That thought at that time would have been bizarre! I had never been on TV before. I was afraid of public speaking, as most people are. I thought perhaps I'd end up with Cheryl and Dean as one of the on-air experts and then I would appear briefly as a testimonial to what they were saying.

But the QVC buyer eventually realized the powerful

story I had to tell and said, no, just YOU.

I met with Cheryl and Dean individually because of their travel schedules. They are entrepreneurial by nature—it's really a mom-and-pop shop—but they care about their product and talk about their herbs as if they're talking about their babies. They are passionate about their product and about helping people lose weight, and their passion certainly rubbed off on me. It's contagious, but I had a real challenge before me: While they could go on and on about an herb for 30 minutes at a clip, I knew if we ever got on the air, I'd have about 10 minutes to describe not only my personal story but the benefits of the product as well. How can I get all this information down to one 10-minute presentation? I had to get down to the key selling points and benefits for the customer—and, as I mentioned, I did this with lots of help from my dad.

Then what happened? When I finally got on the air at QVC that first time, the product sold out in four-and-a-half minutes—before I even got to all the benefits. WHY? Because the viewers had confidence in QVC and in me: If the founder's son was going on the air for the first time with this product—and incidentally, QVC had never offered a diet product before—then people TRUSTED that it must be good and that it must work.

Today we get regular reorders from more than 40,000 people! As you know, I had a real story to tell, and people believed me.

As I've said, I would listen to Dean and Cheryl Radetsky speak of their herbs as lovingly as some parents talk about their children. They would talk for hours about one single herb, explaining why they chose that particular one and how it worked synergistically with the other herbs in Lite Bites.

With their help, I reduced all that information to a few key, easy-to-understand benefits for the QVC viewer. To further my knowledge, I set out on a campaign to learn all I could about herbs, weight loss, and how the human body functions. I must have succeeded because recently, I was at a ski lodge (I can ski a lot better having lost 80 pounds) munching on a Lite Bites bar when someone sitting next to me asked what I was eating.

I pulled out a bar for him to try. I then explained in detail what it was and how it worked, giving him much of the information that I've already shared with you.

I then stopped myself and asked him if I was being too technical. He said no, he was a doctor and he assumed I was one, too. I thanked him for the compliment. It was a pat on the back that we all need once in a while.

—

These days I get a lot of mail from viewers, and I respond to all of it. If it's a real story that people hear, they want to share theirs. I recently heard from one woman who lost 150 pounds. She went from dress size 28 to size 16, and is in her mid 50s. She recently bought herself a snazzy red sportscar. "It's my treat to myself," she wrote me. Like Kathy, whom you met earlier, the first time this woman flew was just recently, because she never could fit into one airline seat! Now, she's invited me to go skydiving with her. It's the new HER! I'm not so sure I'm going to do that, but her enthusiasm for life is contagious and I'm thinking about her invitation.

Another viewer wrote: "I began using Lite Bites approximately ten months ago. At the time I weighed over 300 pounds. To date I have lost 140 pounds, and I credit Lite Bites with helping me to achieve this weight loss. I utilize the Lite Bites bars in various ways, sometimes eating one for breakfast, sometimes using them as a snack in place of a high-fat, high-calorie food. I travel a great deal in my job and do not always have time for a nutritious meal. When I find this happening, I eat a Lite Bites bar for lunch. (I carry a supply of them with me in my car at all times.) I cannot say enough about the Lite Bites products, as I believe they have been a major factor in my achieving my weight loss goal. I plan to continue utilizing these products in the maintenance of my weight loss. I am enclosing a picture of me that was taken at Christmas to show you how I look 'after' Lite Bites."

Another viewer, Cathy from New York, wrote me: "I would like to thank you for bringing such a fantastic product to QVC. I am sending you before and after pictures of my weight loss. My starting weight was 225 pounds in March of 1997. That's when I decided to do something about my weight with the aid of Lite Bites and a healthy eating plan. I have lost 100 pounds. I am down to a much healthier weight for me being only 5'2". And I stand behind your product 100%. Lite Bites and all of the other products work only if you truly have the right mind set and don't consider this a diet, but a healthy new way of life."

As we'll learn in the next chapter, Lite Bites bars work only when you are willing to make them a part of a new, healthier approach to your life that includes a change in attitude, a fitness program, a commitment to low-fat eating, and a willingness to plan your meals and your life to create balance in both.

Here's another Lite Bites success story, this time a letter

from a fan in New Jersey: "I'm sure you've heard it hundreds of times already, but once more won't hurt—I really enjoy your Lite Bites bars! They certainly live up to all the claims you make during your presentations on QVC. Even though I get the Lite Bites bars on autodelivery and am very familiar with your product, I still watch your presentations because you always give some new tidbit of information."

As you'll read in the last chapters of the book, we distinguish between passive and active QVC watchers and what turns a passive viewer into an active one and then, better yet, a buyer. One of the things we strive for is variety: keeping the presentations fresh so viewers will stay tuned. Obviously this fan from New Jersey picked up on the fact that there are always new tips to learn, always new facts to absorb, when using these remarkable Lite Bites products.

With 300,000 bars reordered every single month, Lite Bites is one of the most reordered products on QVC. I'm talking about off-air reorders, which, like a publisher's list of classic books, are the products they don't have to talk up constantly because they just keep on selling themselves. As you have just read for yourself in the responses from users of Lite Bites products, these reorder numbers are hardly surprising.

I've often been asked why Lite Bites hasn't gone retail. Well, for one thing, we simply don't have to. We're doing fine—changing lives—with just the QVC exposure.

I also believe my voice and story help sell the product compared to some product just sitting there on the shelves of some retail store.

In preparation for the next chapter, in which I'll give you more details about the Light Bites Fat-Fighting System, I want you to hear the voices of others who have succeeded with Lite Bites.

Cassandra and Bill from Washington state have appeared with me on QVC a couple of times. Cassie lost 75 pounds and went from a size 24 dress to a size 10. As I've described her on-air, she was once an unhealthy attractive lady and now she's a very healthy attractive lady. In fact, when we were making arrangements for her first appearance, she asked me if the hotel she and Bill would be staying at had an exercise room, because she needed to use the treadmill every day. That was not a statement she would have made 75 pounds ago!

Husband Bill was a typical male. At first he pooh-poohed her Lite Bites bar as just another weight-loss gimmick. Then, at Cassie's insistence, he tried one. They tasted good, so he tried another. Pretty soon, he'd lost 25 pounds without really trying!

Cassie told me recently, "I will probably eat the bars forever! They taste fabulous."

During Cassie's appearance, Teresa from California called in and commented, "I lost 75 pounds with fen-phen, but had to stop using it when the FDA took it off the market. I switched to Lite Bites and, much to my surprise and delight, I continued to lose weight. I've now lost a total of 109 pounds. Believe it or not, I still have a ways to go. Being on the Lite Bites Fat-Fighting System is kind of like eating, but not eating. I just don't feel as hungry as I did before."

Geri Lynn from Minnesota also shared her story with us that evening: "I lost 50 pounds and stopped smoking as a result of the Lite Bites Fat-Fighting System. I felt so good on it that I knew I could finally give up the cigarettes. I haven't lost any more weight—I'm on a plateau—but the good news is that I haven't gained any weight as most people do when they stop smoking. I have really developed a healthy lifestyle and have maintained my weight loss."

Let me highlight a point that Geri Lynn has brought up. It's important to note that most people who do stop smoking gain between 10 and 20 pounds, simply because the body's metabolism slows down once the nicotine is out of the system. Even if they don't eat one additional calorie after stopping smoking, most people gain weight. But Geri Lynn reports that, using the Lite Bites Fat-Fighting System, she was able to stave off that weight gain. That's a great benefit to those of you who are already overweight and are contemplating quitting. You may be hesitant to do so because the last thing you want to do is gain more weight. Here's at least one Lite Bites user for whom weight gain after stopping cigarettes has not been a problem. At Lite Bites, we can't make the claim that it helps ex-smokers prevent weight gain, but anecdotal experience as related to us by Lite Bites users certainly can't be ignored.

Jennifer from New York called in recently and commented, "Every time I want to grab something, I grab a Lite Bites bar. They are such a wonderful product. They are excellent!" We recommend that you eat no more than four servings of Lite Bites a day, but I'm sure Jennifer would be quite full if she ate even that many.

Jo from Texas called in on that same show and reported that she had 50 pounds to lose and was ordering Lite Bites for the first time. I suggested to her that she not think of it as 50 pounds to lose, but to think about losing that first 20 pounds, which seems a lot more achievable. Then, once she's lost those first 20 pounds, she can set a new goal for herself and can approach her ultimate goal more confidently.

Beverly from North Carolina phoned in with this comment; "I lost 30 pounds on fen-phen, but felt miserable every day I took it. Now, I want to do things naturally and with no risk. My weight rebounded after I stopped taking the fen-phen. Lite Bites is a wonderful product and a whole lot cheaper than buying a new wardrobe. I'm a pharmacy technician, so I appreciate the all-natural ingredients found in the bars."

One viewer called in and swore that the Lite Bites bars alleviated the symptoms of rheumatoid arthritis. "I couldn't walk across the room before I started the Lite Bites Fat-Fighting System. Now I've lost weight and can walk quite well, and I believe it's because of Lite Bites."

Obviously, we can't make that claim, just as we can't guarantee that by using Lite Bites bars, you won't gain weight after you stop smoking. But viewers' testimonials to Lite Bites are very convincing and very powerful, and I'm including them here to inspire you to new heights!

One viewer called in with this story: "I went on the Pill two years ago and it caused me to gain a lot of weight. I couldn't go off it, because I needed it for a lot of reasons. My husband was very supportive, told me he loved me no matter what I weighed, but I was just miserable because of the extra weight. Lite Bites was a godsend.

"I don't know why I ordered them when I did. I had been watching QVC for over a year before I ordered, but then a family wedding was coming up and I really wanted to look good. I know there is rigid testing of all products on QVC, so I knew the product was safe. Now my friends are really getting tired of me talking about Lite Bites. I've lost 75 pounds and dropped three dress sizes and I feel just great. The best part is that I've been able to stay on the medication without experiencing the terrible side effects. I have Lite Bites to thank for that."

I could go on and on with Lite Bites success stories. The products have been used by tens of thousands of loyal and satisfied customers. But by now you may want to know about the Lite Bites Fat-Fighting System in more detail, which is in the following chapter.

Let me remind you what I've said throughout these pages about luck, timing, and life. Obviously, in each of the success stories you've just read, something happened to transform that QVC viewer into an enthusiastic Lite Bites user. You have just purchased this book, which I hope you'll view as a stroke of luck. But, as I've said many times, luck doesn't just happen. Luck demands change. The time is now to implement those changes that will affect the rest of your life.

Are you ready to begin?

Chapter Six

The Lite Bites® Way to Lose Weight—and Keep It Off

After Dad handed me that first jar of Lite Bites wafers, I discovered that I had no excuses NOT to lose the weight. In fact, I was SO pleased with the results that I naturally wanted to dig deeper, share my success with others. My natural curiosity drew me to the founders of Lite Bites, Dean and Cheryl Radetsky.

As I said in the previous chapter, I would listen to the Radetskys talk lovingly, passionately, about their herbs, and I had to reduce all that information to a few easy-to-understand benefits for the QVC viewer. But one of the benefits of writing this book is that I have the luxury to go into more detail about how the Lite Bites Fat-Fighting System works in conjunction with the changes you must make in order to succeed in losing weight. What I'm about to reveal to you I can't take credit for, because I'm sharing with you the Lite Bites program that Cheryl and Dean developed themselves for their Lite Bites customers. It's nothing radical—just plain common sense if you're serious about weight loss.

The weight-management material in this chapter is adapted from the *Lite Bites Healthy Lifestyle Book* and used with permission of Optimum Lifestyle, Inc. Copyright © 1998 by Optimum Lifestyle, Inc. All rights reserved.

Of course, it's important to check with your doctor before beginning this or any other weight management or fitness program. Because of factors we can't possibly know concerning your health history, the Lite Bites Fat-Fighting System products may or may not be right for you. Only your doctor or health care provider can give you the go-ahead.

If you've been cleared by your doctor or health care practitioner, there's just one other word of advice: For best results, enjoy Lite Bites products 30 to 60 minutes before meals, or between meals if you'd like. Lite Bites products work best on an empty stomach and when used with this program, the Lite Bites Fat-Fighting System, or other healthy low-fat diet and fitness programs. Do not consume more than four servings of Lite Bites products per day.

The Lite Bites Fat-Fighting System is not one of those quick fix (ha!) "on-again/off-again" diets. Haven't you had enough of those? Instead, it's a way to eat and live more healthfully—every day!

The truth is that you don't need another diet. Diets, as you well know, are only short-term efforts, and as any businessperson can tell you, short-term efforts yield short-term results. Sure, you can get into that smaller size for your class reunion, but will you still be able to do so a month from now? Sure, you may lose a few pounds initially with the newest get-thin-quick effort, but once the deprivation stops, the pounds and inches return. Along with the self-loathing of yet another ride on the diet roller coaster.

If that's what happened to you, you are not alone. Banish any last remnants of guilt from your self-esteem. It happened to me—many times. You are fighting a losing battle . . . literally. I've talked with obesity experts who tell me we have a better chance of hitting it big in Vegas than "hitting it thin" by dieting.

Here's the good news: This is a strategic way to lose extra weight, to stop yo-yo dieting, to put an end to compulsive overeating, and to banish any negative, self-defeating attitudes. How does that sound to you?

The Lite Bites Fat-Fighting System can be your roadmap to living more healthfully (and more happily!) ever after.

Research shows that DIETS DON'T WORK

- Dieting actually lowers your metabolism. This metabolic slowdown continues even after you resume "normal" eating.[1]
- Researchers have found that dieting helps increases the activity of fat-storage enzymes—making it even easier to regain weight.[2]

[1] Elliot DI, et al. Sustained Depression of the Resting Metabolic Rate after Massive Weight Loss (*American Journal of Nutrition,* 1989, 1993).

[2] Kern, PA, et al. The Effect of Weight Loss on the Activity and Expression of Adipose Tissue Lipoprotein Lipase in Very Obese Humans. (*New England Journal of Medicine,* 1990, 322.1053).

Sure, it takes some effort. But once you've mastered these four steps to total mind and body health, you'll find yourself naturally managing your weight . . . without ever wanting to diet again.

These four easy-to-follow steps of the Lite Bites Fat-Fighting System consist of two components for your mind and two components for your body. Together they reinforce a healthy lifestyle that will nourish your whole being. These four components work together to give you the necessary vital elements for long-term success.

The four steps to success are:
- PLANNING
- FOOD
- FITNESS
- ATTITUDE

These four steps are based on a total lifestyle improvement program. There are no temporary stopgaps here, no shortcuts to success. You'll have to customize the program to see what works best for you. We've found that the best way to begin this program is to begin with a plan that has achievable goals.

We'll briefly outline some ideas for planning. For a more complete approach, please see the Lite Bites Healthy Lifestyle Workbook that appears at the end of the book.

It's All In Your Mind!

Those who start off with a "strategy" for losing weight are the most successful. Develop a plan that will work for you. Figure out and write down what your mealtime options are. How will you cope with parties? With that daily plate of danish at the office? Work with your own habits, tastes, and schedules to develop a food and fitness strategy that will work for you.

You've heard me say on QVC a million times: I lost 80 pounds, but I didn't set out to lose 80 pounds. I started first with a strategy to lose 20 pounds, a goal that seemed attainable to me, and, when I accomplished that goal (and felt GREAT about it!), I created a new plan with different, but still workable goals. Let's talk about that.

PLANNING

What are *your* goals? The best advice I can give you is to think in terms of baby steps, as I did. Instead of targeting a 75-pound weight loss, think in terms of the first 5 or 10 pounds. It's a lot easier to build on many small successes than it is to scale a towering mountain in one death-defying leap.

And while I'm giving out advice, let me suggest that you need to be realistic about what is achievable for you. Being supermodel thin is not an ideal that most of us should aim to achieve. And, to be perfectly honest, there's more to life than looking like an anorexic 14-year-old.

• There's feeling healthy and fit.
• There's loving the body you were born with.
• There's eating more healthfully today than you did yesterday.

Remember, the "average" model is 5'10" and weighs 123 pounds. The average American woman is 5'4" and weighs 144 pounds!

You get the idea. So . . . dig out your pencil and dig deep into your motivations for starting this program. Write out your list. This list is what will keep you going when the going gets challenging. Ask yourself these questions—and write down your answers in your Lite Bites Workbook.

First, ask yourself these questions:
• On a scale from one to 10, how committed am I to living more healthfully?
• What are my top three goals for this month?
• If I achieve these goals, how would I like to reward myself with something other than food?

Non-food rewards could include getting a pedicure or seeing a movie you've wanted to see. Be good to yourself. You deserve it!

Following is a sample of how one QVC viewer answered these questions:

On a scale from 1 to 10, how committed am I to living more healthfully?

___10___

My top three goals for this month are:
1. No eating sweets at night.
2. Substitute mustard for mayo in all my sandwiches.
3. Read labels more consistently BEFORE I purchase product.

I will reward myself for reaching these goals, not with food, but with:
1. A new jazz CD with money saved from unnecessary snacks.
2. A phone call late at night to my friend in Oregon when I get the munchies.
3. An extra video rental.

Another viewer showed me her goals:

On a scale from 1 to 10, how committed am I to living more healthfully?

___10___

My top three goals for this month are:
1. Limit chocolate to one small piece per day.
2. Lose two pounds this month. No more, no less.
3. Cut all restaurant entrée portions in half and take the rest home for another meal.

I will reward myself for reaching these goals, not with food, but with:
1. A massage.
2. A facial.
3. The newest romance novel by my favorite author.

You get the idea. The goals are ones YOU set, as are the rewards you get when you reach your goals. Now, take a minute to answer these questions and review *your* goals. Write them down in your Lite Bites Workbook.

FOOD

Walk into any supermarket and you'll see aisle after aisle of low-fat and fat-free everything. There are two things you should know about these choices:

- Get to know what your healthier food options are.
- Let me introduce you to my friend, Mr. Portion Control.

First, let's tackle the FAT.

It's a hard fact to absorb, but it's true: Even fat-free calories count. If I've said it once, I've said it a hundred times on QVC: Any *extra* calories you consume—even fat-free ones —will be stored by your body as fat. Fat-free products usually make up for their lack of taste with that nasty old nemesis, sugar. That means they are high in calories. Don't fall into the trap of thinking that fat-free Devil's Food Cakes won't show up on those hips or at that waistline. Those mouthfuls contain lots of calories, and, at the end of the day, if you aren't expending those calories, they'll be with you for a lot longer than you think.

Fat itself is an even bigger calorie load. Plain and simple, fat makes you fat. At nine calories per gram, fat packs over twice the calorie wallop of either protein or carbohy-drates—both only four calories per gram. A high-fat diet brings with it increased risk of heart disease and cancer— not to mention flabby thighs, a gushy stomach, and that sinking feeling you get when nothing fits.

The Real Cost of Obesity

It is estimated that a 10-pound loss per every overweight U.S. person would reduce the national health bill by $100 billion.

It's true that some fats are better for you than other fats, and it's also true that you do need a bit of fat in your diet every day. (See the following to estimate how much, and ask your doctor if he agrees.) Olive oil (a monounsaturated fat—that means it's liquid at room temperature) is a far better choice than margarine (a saturated fat—that means it's solid at room temperature). However, both are 100% fat, meaning that 100% of their caloric value comes from fat. And fat calories are quickly and easily stored by your body as . . . you guessed it . . . fat!

Most of us eat way too much fat every day—and that's why we are fat. Here are some healthy ways I've found to minimize my fat intake.

MARV'S HEALTHY WAYS TO MINIMIZE FAT

Read every nutritional label. No exceptions. If a label doesn't list the fat content, it's because you wouldn't want to know. Need I say more?

Go fat-free. Switch from ice cream to non-fat yogurt. Sample fat-free dressings, sauces, baked goods, etc. to find the one that tastes like an indulgence rather than cruel and unusual punishment.

Substitute low-fat foods for their higher-fat counterparts. Try mustard on your sandwiches instead of mayo. Try all-fruit jam on your toast or bagel instead of butter or margarine.

Dining out? Specify that you want your entrée broiled

without any oil or butter. Or order it steamed. Most restaurants are very accommodating—they have to be to stay in business. If your dish arrives swimming in a pool of butter, send it back. You deserve better.

Make a list of some ways you can cut fat from your own diet and enter them on page 190 of your Lite Bites Workbook.

SOME SMART SWAPS		
Instead of:	**Have:**	**You save:**
French Fries (3 oz.)	Baked Potato (med.)	14 g fat
Potato Chips (2 oz.)	Pretzel (2 oz.)	18 g fat
Ice Cream (1/2 cup)	Fruit Sorbet (1/2 cup)	7 g fat
Creamy Italian Dressing (1 tbsp.)	Fat-Free Dressing (1 tbsp.)	8 g fat
Caesar Salad	Green Salad w/ fat-free dressing and grilled skinless chicken	30 g fat
Chocolate Croissant	Lite Bites Bar	27 g fat

Now, let me introduce you to Mr. Portion Control.

Let's assume you've been ruthless about trimming the fat. However, if you are still eating enough to satisfy a famished linebacker, you need to know about portions.

Even if you are eating ALL the right things, you cannot consume unlimited quantities of them—and still lose weight. Here's a little trick to figure out how many calories and fat grams you can consume and still lose weight. Take your goal weight for the first 4 to 6 weeks and multiply it by 12. The resulting number is your recommended daily calorie consumption. So, if your goal weight is 150 pounds, and you multiply it by 12, your daily calorie goal would be 1,800 calories. But this is only one part of the equation. The make-up of those calories is very important, especially as they relate to fat grams. How many fat grams do you need every day? This is trickier, but it works:

Take the last digit off your Goal Weight for your minimum. Double that number for your maximum. Example: your Goal Weight is 150 pounds. Take off the "0" to get the number 15. You should limit your daily intake to between 15 and 30 fat grams. Follow this requirement closely. Again, I advise reading the labels on food products and getting a fat gram counter and keeping it with you at all times. Every morsel you eat—yes, even Lite Bites bars—counts against your daily allotment of calories and fat grams. And if you're eating an extra large portion, be sure to take that into account. By the way, restaurant portions of any protein or pasta tend to be at least two to three times a serving size. So, the next time you are eating out, cut those portions in half, eat one half and take a doggy bag home with the rest.

Portion control is an acquired skill. Be patient. It will take a little time—but it will be well worth it. Try to reeducate your eyes (and stomach!) by getting familiar with what a serving size looks like:

1 cup pasta = closed fist
3 oz. protein = deck of cards
1 oz. popcorn = four handfuls
1 oz. potato chips = two handfuls

Use the "1/3 Rule."

For a balanced meal, the protein portion should take up 1/3 of your plate. Vegetables, grains, and fruit should take up the rest.

HOW MANY SERVINGS A DAY?

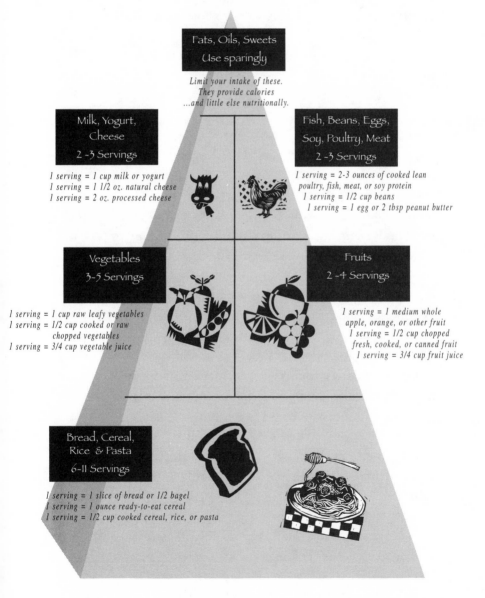

Fats, Oils, Sweets
Use sparingly

Limit your intake of these.
They provide calories
...and little else nutritionally.

Milk, Yogurt,
Cheese

2 -3 Servings

1 serving = 1 cup milk or yogurt
1 serving = 1 1/2 oz. natural cheese
1 serving = 2 oz. processed cheese

Fish, Beans, Eggs,
Soy, Poultry, Meat

2 -3 Servings

1 serving = 2-3 ounces of cooked lean
poultry, fish, meat, or soy protein
1 serving = 1/2 cup beans
1 serving = 1 egg or 2 tbsp peanut butter

Vegetables

3-5 Servings

1 serving = 1 cup raw leafy vegetables
1 serving = 1/2 cup cooked or raw
chopped vegetables
1 serving = 3/4 cup vegetable juice

Fruits

2 -4 Servings

1 serving = 1 medium whole
apple, orange, or other fruit
1 serving = 1/2 cup chopped
fresh, cooked, or canned fruit
1 serving = 3/4 cup fruit juice

Bread, Cereal,
Rice & Pasta

6-11 Servings

1 serving = 1 slice of bread or 1/2 bagel
1 serving = 1 ounce ready-to-eat cereal
1 serving = 1/2 cup cooked cereal, rice, or pasta

The food pyramid illustrates where you should be getting your daily calories. The higher number of servings comes out to about 2,000 calories a day, which is a hearty diet for teenage boys, active men, or very active women. The lower number of servings is more in the ballpark if you're trying to trim a few pounds.

Create your own eating plan.

Why is this so important? Let's review the reasons why most diets fail.

As we noted above, most diets fail because restricting food intake leaves you a metabolic wreck. Why? Because your body, sensing a famine coming on, actually slows up your metabolism to make sure you stay alive through the coming rough times. Exactly what we DON'T need when we diet, but try to tell that to your body, which is made up of genetic material that has survived zillions of years.

But there's another reason why diets fail: As a rule, no one likes being told what they can or can't eat. We all have our own likes and dislikes. Let's face it, some nights you may not feel like having four grapes (count 'em!) for dessert.

In addition, researchers have found that those who were most likely to lose weight—and keep it off—did so by following their own eating plan. The difference? A diet is short-term deprivation. An eating plan is a lifetime lifestyle strategy.

How can you stack the deck for success? Each day, carry a copy of the chart on the next page with you and check off each serving as you go. The chart will help you keep track of what you've eaten and help you plan the rest of your day. *Remember those serving sizes!* One serving is half a bagel or 2 to 3 ounces

Today's Eating Journal

Today's Date: _____

My Top Healthy Lifestyle Goal for this Week: _____

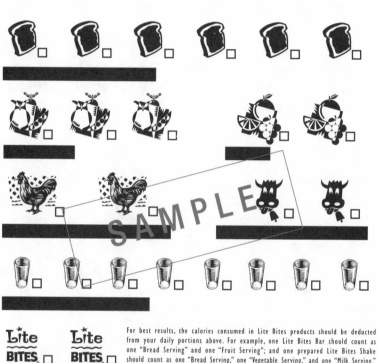

Lite BITES. ☐ **Lite BITES.** ☐   For best results, the calories consumed in Lite Bites products should be deducted from your daily portions above. For example, one Lite Bites Bar should count as one "Bread Serving" and one "Fruit Serving"; and one prepared Lite Bites Shake should count as one "Bread Serving," one "Vegetable Serving," and one "Milk Serving."

Today I felt . . . ☐ great, ☐ okay, ☐ fat, or ☐ _____

My hunger and cravings were . . . ☐ under control, or ☐ wild & ravenous.

What I could do better tomorrow is . . .

_____

_____

of protein—don't assume you can eat like a lumberjack and still lose weight.

If you eat a Lite Bites bar 30 to 60 minutes before a meal, the combination of the nutritional profile with the custom herbal blend and vitamins and minerals go to work in your body to help reduce your hunger level. When you sit down to eat your meal, you are initially still hungry, but you fill up much faster because of the natural action of glycogen signaling that you're full.

SAMPLE MENU CHOICES

Now that you have a blueprint of the foods you should be eating, in the proper proportions, here are a few smart eating choices to get you cookin'.

Breakfast—choose one:
- 2 Lite Bites® Wafers 1/2 hour before breakfast, *if desired*
- Dry cereal with skim milk and berries
- Whole-grain English muffin topped with sliced tomato and fat-free cheese, then broiled in the toaster oven
- Hot oatmeal cooked with apple juice and raisins
- Nonfat yogurt with fresh fruit
- Lite Bites® Bar
- Lite Bites® Fat-Fighting Shake made with skim milk
- Egg or egg substitute with whole-grain toast and fruit conserves
- Corn tortilla filled with scrambled egg or tofu, veggies, and salsa
- Whole-grain French toast made with egg substitute

Late Morning (at least 30 minutes before lunch) — choose one:
- 1 Lite Bites® Bar or 2 Lite Bites® Wafers
- 1 to 2 Lite Bites® Booster Caplets

Lunch — choose one:
- Tuna salad (use nonfat yogurt instead of mayo) on whole-wheat toast with lettuce and tomato
- Pita stuffed with veggies, sprouts, and fat-free cheese, with oil-free dressing
- Split pea soup; fat-free whole-grain crackers; carrot sticks
- Lite Bites® Fat-Fighting System Shake made with skim milk
- Lentil salad on romaine lettuce with fat-free dressing
- Baked potato stuffed with cottage cheese and scallions, topped with broccoli; tomato & basil salad with balsamic vinegar
- Vegetarian chili; fat-free cornbread
- Pasta salad with fat-free Italian dressing and diced raw vegetables

Late Afternoon (at least 30 minutes before dinner)— choose one:
- 1 Lite Bites® Bar or 2 Lite Bites® Wafers
- 1-2 Lite Bites® Booster Caplets

Dinner —choose one:
- Grilled chicken breast or tofu; couscous; steamed vegetables
- Carribean black beans with onions, tomatoes, and spices; brown rice; steamed broccoli; tossed salad with balsamic vinegar

- Broiled fish with nonfat yogurt and Dijon mustard sauce; potato wedges sprinkled with rosemary; steamed spinach
- Shrimp or tofu brochettes; asparagus with seasoned rice vinegar; millet
- Vegetable lasagna made with fat-free cheese; steamed green beans
- Chicken, fish, or bean tacos in 2 corn tortillas; lettuce & spicy salsa
- Skinless chicken breast baked with non-fat French dressing; acorn squash sprinkled with cinnamon; fat-free whole-grain dinner roll

Delectable Desserts — choose one:
- Nonfat frozen yogurt
- Cantaloupe or fruit salad
- Banana with nonfat vanilla yogurt
- Fat-free cookies or crackers
- Fat-free pretzels
- Cinnamon-raisin bagel
- Caramel-flavored rice cakes
- Baked apple
- Fresh strawberries with orange juice and fresh mint
- Lite Bites® Bar
- Lite Bites® Fat-Fighting System Shake (made as hot cocoa)

MARV'S FAVORITE FAT-FIGHTING TIPS

Needless to say, if all we ever craved was steamed broccoli, there wouldn't be any need for me to share these tricks with you. However, these little tidbits have helped me to trim the fat—painlessly!—without feeling deprived. See which ones can help you! (P.S. I'd love to hear from you about your favorite fat-fighting tips. Maybe that'll be my next book: A collection of the best fat-fighting tips from those who know best, those QVC veterans in the field—YOU!)

Breakfast

- Put a half-cup measuring cup inside your cereal box. It will keep you honest about those portion sizes.
- Spread one tablespoon of all-fruit jam, fruit "butter," or nonfat cream cheese on your toast or bagel, instead of butter.
- Order your omelet with egg whites only, instead of whole eggs.

Lunch

- To control the amount of oil you eat with your health salad, ALWAYS order your dressing on the side. Don't drizzle it. Dip your fork into the dressing, then load it up with your bite of salad.
- If you splurge with a burger or a piece of pizza, try blotting its surface with a napkin to soak up some of the grease.
- If you absolutely must have mayonnaise or butter on your sandwich, spread just the tiniest amount around the edges. It will trick your taste buds into feeling satisfied.

Dinner

- Instead of fat-laden garlic bread made with butter, spread baked garlic cloves on French bread.
- Order fajitas instead of enchiladas in a Mexican restaurant.
- Eating out Italian? Skip the alfredo, carbonara, and other creamy sauces in favor of a tomato sauce.

• Grilling vegetables enhances their flavor and uses minimal oil.

In Recipes

- Use potatoes to thicken any soup.
- Replace 1/2 stick of butter in baked goods with two ounces of tofu or an equal amount of prune puree or applesauce.
- Use one cup evaporated skim milk instead of one cup heavy cream in sauces or soups.
- Use rice vinegar or balsamic vinegar instead of wine vinegar in salad dressing. You'll need less oil to balance the acidity.

General Fat-Fighting Tips

- *Avoid very low-calorie diets.* They can promote the loss of lean muscle and promote FAT storage.
- *NO foods are forbidden*—the more you deprive yourself, the more likely you are to binge.
- *Speedy Goals = Speedy Failure.* Set your goals for 1 to 2 pounds per week.
- *Eat more frequently.* 4 to 6 meals per day are much better that 1 or 2 per day. With fewer, larger meals, your body will shut down, and you can actually lower your rate of metabolism.
- *Get mobile: Exercise!* Take a walk, do something more than you did yesterday.
- *Stop watching the scale!* How do you feel? How do your clothes fit? By watching the scale, you could be losing muscle weight, not fat weight.
- *Drink at least eight glasses of water a day.* This is vital! Sometimes when we think we're hungry, we're really

just thirsty. Try a glass of water before reaching for that calorie-filled snack.

FITNESS

The third step to success in the Lite Bites Fat-Fighting System is to develop a regular fitness activity program. Believe it or not, this is the single most important factor for success in long-term weight management.

(Don't do it the way I did it. As I've said, I lost my first 12 pounds without really trying. My dad handed me some of the wafers and suggested that I try them. If they worked, then perhaps I could go on QVC and talk about them. They worked—so well in fact that it wasn't until I had lost 12 pounds that I even realized what was happening. But I still hadn't started a fitness routine. I couldn't! I was so heavy I was convinced that I would have had a heart attack. Things are different now, and I have a strenuous routine I'm committed to three or four times a week. My routine varies. I work out at a gym for 30 minutes on machines, such as the Stairmaster, that improve my cardiovascular system. If the weather's bad, I'll use a ski machine I have in my basement and then do 20 to 30 pushups and about 50 situps at a time. I do these activities several times a week. But what I really love is to be outdoors and mountain bike, horseback ride, golf, or ski. I feel great having lost 80 pounds—so far! The lesson here is the sooner you get to it, the sooner you'll feel great, too!)

So, how do you get started?

- *Get up and go!* It may seem obvious, but it needs to be stated—simply get up off the couch or that comfy chair and start moving! It's that easy! You don't need any expensive equipment or a gym membership . . . just a little motivation. If you usually take elevators, go for the stairs. Get off the bus a few blocks from your office—or park your car at the farthest corner of the lot. Give up your membership in the CPA (Couch Potatoes of America). Moving around feels great, it does wonders for your self-esteem, and, as research shows, you'll be more likely to keep your weight off.

- *Do what you love.* Find a fitness activity you truly love—and make it a part of your lifestyle. I really love golf and try to do it every single day. Recently I was introduced to horseback riding. You wouldn't believe how many calories you burn up doing two or three hours in the saddle! But don't just think of what activity will burn off the most calories in the least amount of time. Choose an exercise or an activity you truly love and make it part of your life.
- *Burn, baby, burn!* Give your metabolism an extra boost by working out. Develop an exercise routine that you do at least three times a week. Exercise burns up calories during your workout—and for up to 18 hours afterward!
- *Doctor's okay.* Reminder: Check with your physician or health care provider before beginning any fitness or weight-loss program.

To get started, just keep these pointers in mind:
- Exercise at least three to five times per week.
- Warm up for 7 to 10 minutes before you begin your routine.
- Maintain a moderate workout level for 30+ minutes.
- If you are new to working out, 15 minutes at first is fine.
- Gradually cool down your activity for 2 to 3 minutes.
- Include post-activity stretches for 5 minutes.

Keep track of your fitness activities by keeping a diary such as this one. You can make your own activities chart on page 196 in the Lite Bites Healthy Lifestyle Workbook.

Here are some fitness activities I can easily start this week (after I check with my doctor):

Walk after dinner

Take stairs instead of escalator

Go swimming once a week at the Y

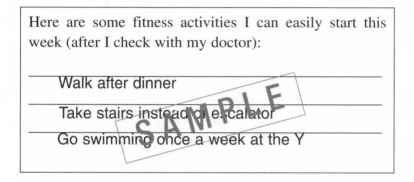

Many studies have shown that continuing to exercise after losing weight is the best predictor of keeping the weight off. The strongest predictor of weight gain? Watching TV (except for QVC, of course!).

In a study of nearly 17,000 people, those who regularly exercised tended to live longer—as much as two years longer—than those who didn't!

ATTITUDE

Did you ever use eating as "the Great Escape?" As I related in earlier chapters, I sure did. Well, if you're "fed up" with food getting the best of you (as I eventually was), this section is for you.

Breaking out of "the Great Escape" habit can be challenging, to say the least. The bad news is that you'll have to say no to old habits and immediate gratification. I had to say goodbye to those big bowls of colorful M&Ms I used to enjoy. And to my morning danish (or two!). But the good news is that making the escape from the Great Escape will make all the difference in the world to your health—and to your self-esteem.

The key is to develop your Conscious Eating Plan. Going through the following steps every time you eat will shift eating from being the Great Escape to being a very real, very conscious pleasure. Trust me on this one. Be especially careful when eating out with another person or a group.

A ccording to a recent study, people seem to develop eating amnesia when dining with others. Eating in a group of six or more increased their food consumption by 76%! Eating with just one other person boosted consumption by 28%!

Here's a Marv tip: Use eating out as a chance not to gorge, but to eat much healthier. Think of it—someone else is doing the cooking and the cleaning up, so you can really order anything you want prepared just the way you want it. Sometimes at home, I am too tired to fix a salad for dinner or a fruit plate for dessert. In a restaurant, you can have someone do that for you. Think about it!

Develop your Conscious Eating Plan.

Follow these steps every time you think you are hungry—you'll be amazed at the results.

- Before eating anything, take a deep breath while counting to four. Hold it to the count of four. Now exhale to the count of four. Do this four times. This exercise will help you "be in the moment," instead of unconsciously inhaling an entire plate of food without even "checking in" to find out what you really need to eat (if anything).

- Now ask yourself this question and be honest with your answer: 'Am I hungry?' If your answer is yes, ask yourself, 'What for?' Food? Or something else, like connection with someone? Or relief from boredom? Become aware that hunger isn't just for food.
- If it is for food, ask 'What will satisfy me?' By following your "internal cues," you will be able to truly feel satisfied by what you choose to eat.
- Now eat s-l-o-w-l-y. Taste each bite. Chew each mouthful, paying attention to all of the sensations. Stay present with the act of eating.
- Notice when you are beginning to feel full, and STOP EATING.

What causes eating binges? Many experts believe that dieting causes bingeing. However, some foods or situations, such as family gatherings, may be "binge triggers" for you. Make a list of your "binge triggers." Write them down in your workbook. Be specific about the situations and the foods that cause them. List all the foods you know you can't keep in the house because they "call" to you until you've eaten every single morsel! Keep those foods out of your home. Consume them only in small quantities outside the confines of your abode!

What would be alternate ways of handling these binge situations? Make a list of ten ways to handle difficult food situations, beginning with: Commit 100%. No, make that 110%.

Success starts in your mind. Make a conscious decision—right now—to fully commit yourself to this program and reach your goals. *This is the single most important step you can take right now.*

Don't use food as the Great Escape.

Yes, we all know that food works as a great escape. But you'll pay a price—on your waistline . . . on your hips . . . on your heart. Discover some healthy ways to de-stress. Make a list that begins, "When I'm stressed out, instead of mindless munching, I can go for a walk. . . ." and enter it in the Attitudes section of your Lite Bites Workbook.

MORE OF MARV'S FAT-FIGHTING TIPS

Why do we think that food equals love?

As children, what happened when we were upset? If your Mom was anything like mine, she gave you a cookie. We felt loved. How about when we were feeling hurt? Usually, another cookie. Lonely? Uh-huh. What about when we got a gold star on our homework and felt happy? When we got home from school, Mommy gave us—another cookie.

It's easy to see how our brains may have figured out that whenever we feel any emotion, what we should do to handle it is—eat more cookies. List the ways you use food to cope with feelings and enter them in your workbook.

Avoid all-or-nothing thinking.

Whoops! Okay, you fell off the wagon, forgot your Conscious Eating Steps, and ate that entire pint of Double Dutch Rocky Road Mocha Fudge. (What was it doing in your freezer in the first place?) Don't feel that you've blown the whole program. Just get right back to eating healthfully. Check your workbook frequently.

Keep a food diary.

What's the best way to keep track of your daily binge triggers and other unconscious cues that signal your eating?

You guessed it! A food diary! It will help you pinpoint which eating behaviors leave you feeling your best . . . and which can be improved. A sample can be found in the Lite Bites Workbook.

If you find you're eating a pizza (or two) every time you feel anxious, or you tend to feel tired and sluggish after you have "the usual" for lunch, you can experiment with other strategies to find what will work better for you.

That pretty much sums up the Lite Bites Fat-Fighting System. It's a lot of common sense mixed with a lot of commitment to reach goals you set for yourself. It's not always easy, but it can be done. Just remember the four steps to success: planning, food, fitness, and attitude. And remember to use your workbook as an important tool to achieve your healthy lifestyle goals.

Scrapbook
My Personal History

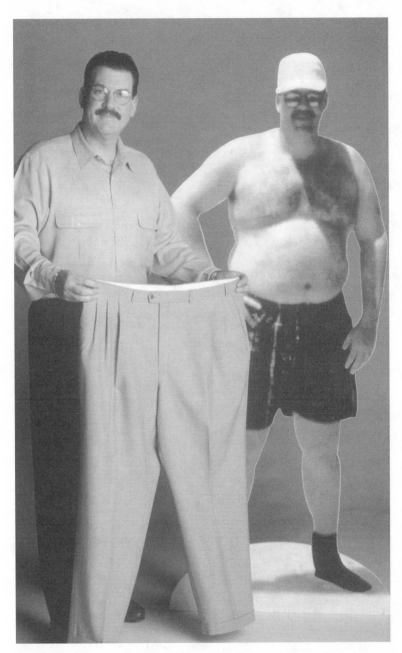

Here I am next to my cutout, Big Marv, and with the size 46 pants I used to wear. Both are excellent visual aids in showing on-air how well the Lite Bites Fat-Fighting System works.

My father, Joe Segel, and I, engaged in conversation at a cocktail party. He was probably giving me some sound business advice.

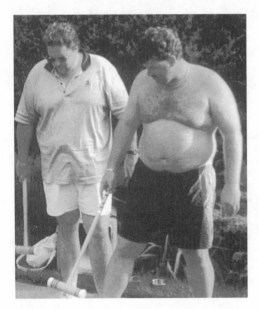

Senior year of high school, 1973. Under all that hair is close to 300 pounds of me, mostly body fat.

Scary, isn't it? That's me on the right. The technicians in the sound booth at QVC like to ask me whether I wore a B or C cup at this time, a line I've used many times on the air. With me is my equally chubby cousin, Ben Keogh, who had the sense to keep his shirt on.

My father and Doris.

My mother, with her
husband, Irv.

Kathy Fodge, as she appeared on our January 10, 1999, broadcast. Kathy lost 150 pounds in two years, going from a size 28 to a size 8. A Missouri resident, she first appeared on QVC on September 17, 1998, and took her first plane ride to get to the studios. (She never before fit into one airline seat!) "I tried every weight-loss product in the book," she said. "They'd work for a while and then they just didn't work anymore.... The great part about Lite Bites is that they now help me maintain my weight. That's why I agreed to a return appearance on QVC."

116

Cassandra and Bill Stephani from Washington state make their second appearance for the Lite Bites Fat-Fighting System on January 10, 1999. Cassie lost 75 pounds, trimming her figure from a size 24 to a size 10. Husband Bill, whom I like to call a "typical male," pooh-poohed her Lite Bites bars at first, then he tried one, then another and another, and lost 25 pounds with very little effort. Today he's a fan of the Lite Bites Fat-Fighting System. Says Cassie, "I'll probably eat the bars forever. They taste fabulous!"

The founders of Lite Bites, Cheryl and Dean Radetsky.

Ben Keogh in leaner times, on the January 10, 1999, broadcast. He lost 45 pounds using the Lite Bites Fat-Fighting System.

Above right: Cathy Palmeri, as she appeared on our first live-audience broadcast January 10, 1999. She went from a size 22 to a size 2 using the Lite Bites Fat-Fighting System.

Right: Julie Carson, as she appeared on our first broadcast before a live audience. Using the Lite Bites Fat-Fighting System, Julie lost 45 pounds in six months, shedding seven inches off both her waist and hips and dropping three dress sizes. "Chewies are so good, I call them my license to cheat."

118

Here I am with my horse, Sampson.

Part Three
Making It at QVC

Chapter Seven

Why We Hate Commercials but Love QVC

Well, by now you certainly know enough about my life and about the forces and factors that brought me to QVC—my weight problem, the influence of my dad, my introduction to and then use of Lite Bites products, my success in losing weight by following the Lite Bites Fat-Fighting System, and, finally, my success in bringing Lite Bites to QVC and representing the product on the air. I have truly been blessed, not only by the good fortune I've encountered along the way, but also by the people whose lives have changed for the better using the Lite Bites products and have gone to considerable effort to tell me so.

The remaining chapters of the book are my attempt to take you behind the scenes at QVC. I will try to give you a brief glimpse into what really goes into getting a product on the air. Hint: It's not as easy as it may appear on your television screens. I think this information will be valuable because many of you, I'm sure, believe that you are the next Thomas Alva Edison, that you've invented a better light bulb or mousetrap or whatever it is that gets you up in the morning and keeps your creative juices going all day. Some of the information will be practical in nature, some of it merely informative, some of it examples of others who have done it.

Let's begin with an overview of QVC.

As I mentioned in the introduction, QVC stands for Quality, Value, Convenience—three concepts that are difficult to achieve in traditional retailing today. Here's why my father got the idea for QVC and why it's been such a big hit with consumers.

Electronic retailing was bound to come along sooner or later. The technology has been there, well, since the beginning of television. QVC, therefore, was a giant just waiting to be born. What hastened its delivery, however, was something that practically all of us face every day when we pay a visit to the mall. Remember sales people? What happened? Where did they go? They're certainly not there when you need them.

There's nobody around when you've finally picked out the perfect blouse, or suit, or lampshade, or whatever.

A while back I happened to be talking to a saleswoman who used to work for Strawbridge and Clothier, a major department store in Philadelphia. She told me about a customer who came in with a complaint—when who should be walking by but Mr. Strawbridge himself!

He invited the customer up to his office, straightened everything out, made her feel like a million bucks, and gained a customer for life.

In fact, that kind of personalized service and concern was what gave rise to that American phenomenon, the department store. You could get almost anything you wanted, with an army of salespeople at the ready.

But times certainly have changed.

Let's pretend that the last time you went shopping, miracle of miracles, you actually could find help. But—you have a question. For example, does this dress come in your size? Or, does the lawnmower you've picked out work in high grass?

Well, good luck. Usually you're getting the person who's just filling in for the fulltime clerk who's on a break, out to lunch, or on vacation. The manager? The manager is in a meeting.

Even if you overcame all those obstacles, that is, you actually found someone to wait on you, and that person properly explained and demonstrated the product that you're prepared to buy, chances are it's out of stock.

That doesn't happen at QVC. As soon as a product is sold out, QVC announces that fact immediately and pulls it off the air. When the product is back in stock at their warehouses, then it's offered on-air once again.

As consumers, we're starved for information. We want to know what we're buying. You might even say we have a right to know, since it's our money on the line.

That's the theory, but it's just not working out that way anymore. To be blunt about it, traditional retail isn't doing the job.

All right, now let's turn to TV for a moment. You're home, relaxing with your favorite sitcom, and just before the situation resolves itself through comedy—cut! Time for a commercial. You're not a happy camper. You're annoyed. You did not tune in for the commercials. Time for the mute button.

Even if you do stay tuned for the 30-second spot, are you getting the information you need to make an informed buying decision?

Now it's true that not all commercials are uninvited

guests into our homes. During the Super Bowl, we actually look forward to the commercials—not because they're informative and really sell the product, but because they're entertaining.

Now wouldn't it be great if we could be informed and entertained at the same time!

Wouldn't it be terrific if we could flip on the TV and find a virtual mall right before our eyes, and better yet, find people who are not out to lunch—people who actually know the product, have used it or even invented it, and can demonstrate it to you thoroughly?

Welcome to QVC!

At QVC, the men and women who present the product are the show. But the product is the star. The host and the guest provide the "plot" and do so in an informative and entertaining manner.

That, in a nutshell, is the secret to QVC's success and explains why people hate commercials but love QVC.

With all the junk on network TV, QVC offers a refreshing respite. Call it "alternative" television. I call it the background music of the 90s. It's soothing, it's comforting, it's live 24 hours a day. Even when I do an overnight appearance, I can still count on testimonial calls at three or four in the morning. I mean you've got real people talking to you right now, and that's a rarity in itself. And just as important, there's no pressure.

QVC does not sell. The word "sell" is a no-no at QVC. Product after product is presented for your inspection. If you're not interested, fine. Enjoy the patter. If you are interested, terrific. Stay tuned and you'll have enough information to make an intelligent decision as to whether the product is right for you.

It's been my experience that QVC viewers are generally well-educated and prepared to be informed.

We're dealing with a population that tunes to QVC to be informed and entertained, while at the same time being presented with news about products, not people. What I'm saying is that even the six o'clock and six-thirty news have become turn-offs for so many people. Enough with all those shootings and killings and partisan politics.

So much of TV is saturated with gossip, sex, and violence that it's no wonder people have been tuning out of that but tuning into QVC. Network viewership has been declining for years, while QVC's viewership has been on the rise.

There must be a reason. It's more than mere background music.

QVC's unique charm is its ability to present new products hot off the assembly line. For example, when the APS camera was first offered to the public, QVC had a representative from Kodak on the air to explain the ins and outs of this revolutionary breakthrough of photography. I'll bet your local camera shop didn't have that!

Stated simply, QVC viewers are after information, the kind of information they do not get during a 30-second commercial, or during an impatient wait in a department store.

Here's another example that shows how an on-air "demonstrated" product has it all over an item that just sits on the shelf. On December 7, 1996, Packard Bell 200 MHz Pentium Processor computers sold out in just over 20 minutes of QVC airtime. That's $8.2 million worth of business. Who can beat that?

Or this? On any given month, QVC adds more than 150,000 new customers. These people may have been watching QVC for a while just to pass the time, but eventually they learn to trust QVC. QVC earns this trust in many different ways, but testimonials play a major role in making viewers feel more comfortable.

There's another reason viewers feel so comfortable with QVC. In a phrase—risk-free purchases. If you don't like what you bought, just return it, no questions asked. Moreover, given QVC's middle name—value—it's unlikely that the product you purchased will ever be available from another source at a lower price.

On-air spokespersons like myself come across as being extremely credible and knowledgeable because we are connected with the product. It's a requirement. We live and die with the product, and if we backslide even for moment, we're done and the product is finished.

Actually, given QVC's strict adherence to quality assurance standards, there is absolutely no chance of making it in front of the camera unless you're 100% reliable.

The typical lack of professional help at most retail and department stores makes people yearn for demonstrated good information on products. That's assuming you can find anybody to wait on you at all.

The reason we hate commercials is because commercials interrupt what we're trying to watch—and we are not prepared to be sold.

People tune to QVC because of the friendly banter as opposed to the violence and nonsense on the other channels. They buy from QVC because their interest gets aroused when they hear of something that is of value to them.

Hey, I just realized something. I sound like a commercial for QVC.

Sorry, but it is my bread and butter, and I am sold on the place.

As I keep saying, QVC changed my life. It certainly changed the buying habits of millions of Americans. In fact, it changed the very concept of retailing, dramatically so.

I simply would not be honest with myself, or with you, if I denied the fact that I'm a big fan.

Yes, I'm big on QVC—fortunately, with the help of Lite Bites, not nearly as big as I used to be.

———

QVC is seen in more than 60 million homes and, on average, ships out one and a half packages every second. This amounts to 160,000 packages a day—packages that could range from a pair of gold earrings to a computer to a set of pots and pans to a book or a carton of Lite Bites bars. Wow! On average, 20 to 40 thousand new viewers tune into QVC each week. In 1998, QVC did over $2.4 billion in sales, which makes this electronic retail giant bigger than most department stores. It makes QVC bigger than Bloomingdale's and Saks Fifth Avenue. In just one single day, QVC has taken orders for over $20 million.

It's enormously gratifying to see the tears of happiness of small business owners whose lives may change positively as a result of sharing their product and their story on QVC for the first time. It's a rush to be in the Green Room, the private office suite for the guests waiting to go on-air and their families, when a newly introduced product becomes a runaway success. A good example of this phenomenon is that of LitterQuick cat litter boxes. Its proprietors, Jim and Amy Sage, were selling about five hundred litter boxes a year, but had big dreams. Amy was the manager of the gym where I regularly worked out, and one day approached me with her idea of how to sell these litter boxes. They'd had some success at cat shows and by selling directly through ads in cat fancier magazines, but they had already invested in the molds to make many more boxes than they were selling now.

Amy was very passionate about her product and described to me the features and the benefits of this unique litter box, namely, that they are made of plastic that does not absorb any cat odors, and that they are big enough for the average cat. Most cats are 16" long; traditional litter boxes are 12" to 14" long. What does the cat do with the rest of its body?

She and Jim were so committed to their product that I decided to represent them to help them get on QVC. Amy demonstrated how strong the boxes were by standing on one of them, and we made the joke on-air that only a trained professional like her should attempt this feat! Then Jim prepared an overlay to show how much larger the LitterQuick box is than conventional litter boxes—and the host quipped that, indeed, size does matter!

The presentation was very successful, and, as you'll learn later, we were able to monitor that success right there that day in the Green Room—the first time the LitterQuick litter boxes were presented on QVC, more than 2,000 litter boxes were sold at $22 (plus shipping and handling) in just 10 minutes! That's $44,000 in sales for QVC. That's quite a step up from 500 boxes per year. The Sages have since given up their jobs and relocated to be nearer to their production plants so that they can keep a closer eye on their booming business.

Ironically, on that same day, another of my clients went on the air with black pearl jewelry. Black pearls are unique: they grow only in Tahiti because of the water temperature and the kind of plankton available as food for the oyster. It takes the oyster two years to make one pearl, so these particular pearls are quite rare. Now jewelry does not usually need a connected spokesperson—it sells because people think it's pretty or a good value, but not because someone gets pleasure out of wearing it. But in this case, the proprietor was able to show a live oyster with a black pearl inside it. That's the kind of presentation that turns passive viewers into active ones, those who really pay attention to what's being presented on the screen. We pointed out that a pearl is the only product made by nature that is not polished or cut like other gems: it's perfect the way it is. This demo was so effective that the product sold out in record time!

This was a very satisfying day for Segel Associates, the marketing consulting firm I had set up to handle situations like these. I had two clients whose products were hits on the same day.

That's the power of QVC. Come along with a great product, and you might just be in. Not that it's as easy as one-two-three. But I will take you step by step through the different stages, from the moment you first walk in the door at QVC, to going on-air for the first time. But let's not get ahead of ourselves.

Do you ever sit at home watching QVC and think, 'Gee, I just know that my idea about ????? would make a great product to sell on the air'? Have you built a better mousetrap? Developed a better cleaning product? Invented a new way to do your laundry?

Then there's the family who wondered why all the flavor of a chicken never got into the meat. You rub spices onto the skin and then cook the chicken, but who eats the skin anymore? When the skin is peeled off, all you have left is the meat, which has very little of the spicy flavor. Reece Williams still demonstrates on-air the product developed by his late father, who decided to do something about this waste of marinade, and came up with the Cajun Injector. It looks like a huge hypodermic needle filled with Cajun (or any other kind of) spices, which are injected directly into the meat of the chicken. This product demonstrates beautifully on the air (more about that later) because when you start carving the meat, the juices look scrumptious with all the colorful spices running through them.

And what about Cactus Jack? He always wondered why everyone paid for and then lugged home cleaning products that are 99% water. Water out of your tap is pretty nearly free, and you don't have to carry it for miles to its final resting place in your home. So he invented cleaning products that are solid. You add your own water! This isn't brain surgery, folks! This is common sense and Cactus Jack has made a fortune!

What's your good idea? What keeps your internal batteries charged day and night? What kind of a mousetrap are you thinking of building?

In the following chapters, I'm going to explain in detail the inner workings of QVC, how these dreamers and other entrepreneurs got their products on the air—and how you can, too! I'll share with you the successes—and the stumbles—I've had in helping to bring other products to the electronic airways.

Think of this section of the book as the bit of luck that has dropped into your life if this is the right time for you to become a successful QVC product sponsor. But, as I've said before, with luck comes the requirement to change. What you do with the wealth of information in the following pages is up to you, but it just might change your life. It has for me and for thousands of other QVC entrepreneurs.

Chapter Eight

What Products Sell on QVC—and Why

Everybody's an expert—after the fact. If only we could be as smart ahead of time. Take those mavens on the evening news, for example. They're terrific at telling you what happened, and why it happened, why the market went up or down. If they could be so smart in the MORN-ING, now that would be news!

The point is, nobody is that smart, even at QVC. Yes, there's expertise involved—QVC's buyers and planners are paid to anticipate which products will sell. But nobody knows for sure. If they did, they would be multimillionaires and retired. A little luck and timing help.

QVC has got hundreds of buyers and planners jockeying products and airtime to find the perfect match—and it is amazing how many times things do click.

What I'm going to tell you is what formula has worked for me and, just as important, what hasn't worked for me. Yes, as you know by now, I've been pretty successful at QVC, but I am a negative two for two on products that were presented without on-air guests. There's a message here, especially if you're making product claims. If a product demonstrates well by itself, a guest may be optional.

Frequently jewelry items don't need an enthusiastic wearer of them to sell well. But for almost everything else, a connected on-air spokesperson is essential.

Take the case of Joy Mangano and her better mop. She brought the product to a QVC buyer and the buyer was convinced. This mop truly was a great improvement over any mop you can buy in the store. It didn't splinter or rust as most mops do—it was made of plastic. The mop was then aired with the QVC host demonstrating how it worked. And it worked just fine. I mean, really! How hard it is to demonstrate a mop? But guess what happened? The mop just sat there in the warehouse, taking up valuable space and NOT moving. But Joyce and the buyer didn't give up. They gave it one more shot, this time with Joyce herself going on-air not only to demonstrate how the mop worked, but to explain how it was better than the mop you already own. And how she herself recognized the need for this mop. And guess what? The phones lit up—no doubt in response to her personal story—and the product has been a success on QVC ever since. We'll read a bit more about Joy and her mops a bit later.

Clearly, the message is this: It takes two to tango—an interviewer and an on-air guest. The effective way to convey the QVC-approved benefits to the viewer is by having the guest take the interviewer's questions and respond with excitement and passion.

MARV'S FOUR BASIC RULES FOR PROBABLE SUCCESS
1. A great product. Do you have a true problem-solving product?
2. A great story (List the product's 10 key benefits—more about this later).

3. A great demo—the product demonstrates well on-air.
4. A credible spokesperson, who either
   (a) created the product, or
   (b) uses the product professionally, or
   (c) personally uses the product, or
   (d) is otherwise involved with the product.

If you address all four Basic Rules, your product should do well. You can still do okay with two or three of these, but at a minimum you need points 1 and 2.

Years of experience have taught me that a product will have an uphill struggle if it goes on without a spokesperson and does not demonstrate well on-air. At QVC there's very little time to make corrections once a product is introduced and subsequently flops. It does happen that a product can be reintroduced, like Joy's mop that just cried out for her personal touch. But generally, a struggling product's life cycle is fleeting at QVC.

An electronic flare for automobiles is an example of what I've been talking about. I suggested this product to QVC because I loved this product, even bought one for my wife to keep in her car in case the car ever broke down or she got into trouble. What made this flare so special was that it was battery operated, so that when you used it, there was no chance of a spark igniting leaking gasoline or fuel. To the best of my knowledge, it was the only product of its type.

QVC's buyer agreed, saw its benefits, and bought it. It went on-air and died. Why? All it did on-air was blink, and it didn't blink well either because TV studios are brightly lit, so bright, in fact, that the viewer at home can hardly see anything that merely blinks! So the product didn't demonstrate well, and there was really no way to reposition it so that it would. Another key reason for its failure is that it had no connected spokesperson to interact with it. I loved the product, but I will only go on-air with Lite Bites in order to maintain my personal story of success with the product, and with items related to Lite Bites, such as this book.

No one knows your product better than you do.

Soon enough the product was sent off with those three dreaded initials, RTV. That's short for Return to Vendor, and those are words you hate to hear. But as a vendor, at least you're getting your goods back, with some input as to why your product didn't work.

All was not lost. This vendor of the flare learned a valuable lesson and should be better prepared for the next product he brings to QVC. Yes, it's never one or two strikes and you're out at QVC. Remember, QVC is always hungry for new product, and past failures are quickly forgotten. When QVC's buyer makes that tough phone call to return an unsold product, the best vendors ask first why it didn't succeed. Remember, this is not a time to get defensive. Joy Mangano didn't. It was time to learn—learn from her mistakes.

I suggest you pose these questions:
- Was it priced properly?
- Was it a good value?
- Was it properly demonstrated?
- Was the airtime properly produced? Did you or QVC miss some key selling benefits? Were there any bad camera angles? Did any pre-produced videotapes not run? During a live show, strange things happen.

Let's talk a bit more about how products do sell on QVC. Think of QVC as background music for the home in the 90s. How do you transform the listener into a viewer who becomes a buyer for your product?

The sequence to success is as follows:
- Passive listener (QVC is background music for the home)
- Active listener (something you just heard on TV got your attention)
- Active viewer (you like what you've heard and now you want to see what it's about)
- Buyer (you've made the call)

Here are my five points for getting the listener's attention:
1. A premiering product
2. An item available only on QVC
3. A special value
4. Great chemistry with the QVC viewer (you are a natural, honest person and it shows on-air)
5. An exclusive QVC configuration (an item that exists in traditional retail, but by repackaging it or by mating it with another similar product, you have created a product exclusive for QVC)

Remember this is television, so it's not just the product that counts, it's the presentation. As an on-air guest, your job is to be informative, but not boring. Think of yourself as doing improv. It doesn't hurt to spice up your presentation with some entertainment and creativity. That's what Cactus Jack does when he presents his waterless cleaning products. He dresses up like a cowboy who's just arrived from the dusty prairie. It's shtick—the West Chester, Penn., offices are a long way from the heartland—but it works because it grabs the home viewer's attention. It turns that viewer from a passive listener into an active one.

Take my case. After doing an effective presentation with Lite Bites for over a year using my old baggy jacket and pants to show-and-tell the Old Marv versus the New Marv, I found that I could be even more effective if I went back in time. I found an old photo of me on a beach in a bathing suit. I weighed over 300 pounds, a pretty scary sight. The technicians before airtime wanted to know whether I had worn a B or C cup at that time in my life. It's a pretty funny line that I've used again and again on the air.

I used this photo to dramatically present a product benefit, that is, the ability of Lite Bites to help me change my appearance so that I now have no qualms about being photographed at the beach.

Once you have a successful product on QVC, your next tough challenge is keeping your presentation fresh, while still conveying the same benefits. We're getting ahead of ourselves, of course, because there are many steps along the way before a product is deemed a success. But in my experience, the same viewer who failed to be captivated by your noontime presentation may just hear something different from you later in the day and phone in.

For example, during one Lite Bites Today's Special Value, there were a number of occasions when live callers said, "I watched you earlier, but now decided to give Lite Bites a try."

Here's what turned them around. While doing eight appearances that day, one of the producers told me that when I poured the box of Lite Bites Chewies into a bowl, they overflowed, and the phone lines lit up. This overflow was accidental: The staff provided me with a bowl that was too small to hold all the Chewies in the box. But it showed that once viewers understood visually what Chewies were and how many were in this box, their interest was triggered. They saw they were getting good value for their money.

Remember, QVC is a visual medium. Merely saying that there were over a hundred Chewies in a box was not as effective as pouring them in a decent-sized bowl and having them overflow. As the day went on, I would do this demonstration at least twice during each presentation—and each time, the phones lit up.

I know it doesn't seem like much, just pouring those Chewies into a bowl, but believe me, something visual like that can (and did) make all the difference. So I cannot say it often enough—QVC is a visual medium and the act of demonstrating a product is crucial.

Here's another example of the importance of being visual and interacting with your product. On that same show, in order to demonstrate that seven Chewies equal one gram of fat, I simply placed seven Chewies in my hand, held them up to the camera, and said, "Just imagine, you can eat all these, and they all amount to no more than one gram of fat."

Remember, the information can be very dry or it can be very entertaining. Keep it fresh and imaginative. This is television.

Remember the Sages and their LitterQuick litter box? There are many, many varieties of litter boxes on the market. Why does this one sell? Because of its unique features (size, strength, nonabsorption of odors) and because of the connected spokesperson (or in this case, persons!) and a great on-air presentation. The Sages really believe in their product, and their enthusiasm just bubbles through the air-ways and into viewers' homes.

It's hard to predict what will sell and what won't sell on QVC. That's the power of electronic retailing. Who knew that a handcrafted wood figurine of a moose that dispensed candy out its backside would be such a hit? What could the QVC planner possibly have been the thinking when he dared to put this poplar wood item on the air? All I can think was that it must have really hit the right funny bone when the sample first appeared. Yet this item, as wacky as it is, has sold out almost every time it's been on-air.

You probably remember the Arctic 180 ear warmers if you're a regular viewer. They were developed by a business student, Brian Legette, at The Wharton School of Business as part of a course project in retailing. He brought his idea to QVC simply because the studios are located close to Wharton, and millions of ear warmers later, he learned his greatest lesson in the world of business: the business of electronic retailing.

One of my favorite ideas is really a very simple one and one most people can relate to. Most of us have dealt, at one time or another, with shower curtains that take forever to hang because of all those hooks that never seem to want to cooperate with our tired shoulders and hands. Someone did something about that and invented a beautiful shower curtain that does not need hooks. Yes, Teddy Marcus brought us the hookless shower curtain! A big success on QVC.

I hope you are getting the message loud and clear: No matter what your interests, no matter what your taste, there is a product for you to buy from QVC, and there's a product for you to try out on the air. It's impossible to predict what that next successful product will be.

The Power of Electronic Retailing

Because of the success I had with selling Lite Bites on-air, many people have come to me for advice about how to position their products. I've developed a good business advising people whose products I believe in about the most effective way to present that product on-air. And the greatest thrill for a product representative such as myself is to take a small mom-and-pop company and expose it to the power of QVC.

Lite Bites, which first appeared on QVC's second channel, Q2, January 11, 1996, is a classic example of what impact QVC can have on the sales of a company in a very short period of time. Prior to its electronic retailing, Lite Bites had annual sales of $500,000 a year. In 1997 QVC's sales of Lite Bites were in excess of $10 million.

LitterQuick is another product that I represent. As you know from my previous comments, LitterQuick was developed by a husband and wife who owned cats and wanted a litter box that was both cat and people friendly. I mentioned earlier Amy Sage, the manager of a gym where I worked out at regularly. She knew I was on QVC and one day mentioned that she and her husband had this product and wanted my thoughts on it. Three months later, more than 20,000 LitterQuick boxes were sold on QVC.

Such is the power of electronic retailing.

A product that would otherwise just be sitting on a shelf now has a voice through its creator. There is also another factor that leads to success. Luck and timing. One day you're in the gym, and the manager strolls over and asks your opinion about a product—well, need I say more? Yet another example of luck and timing that changed someone's life, even mine!

That relationship with Amy and Jim Sage led to my introduction to the importer of Fresh Magic Cat Litter. At that time the product had not yet appeared in this country.

The Sages and the importer of Fresh Magic, Karen Cohen, had adjoining booths at a cat show. They talked. The next thing you know, I was representing Fresh Magic Cat Litter, a new silica-based cat litter with some unique benefits.

But this product presented a unique challenge. How do you demonstrate the profound benefits of this slippery kitty litter without grossing out the audience? I'd thought of using Baby Ruth bars or Tootsie Rolls, but even I thought that was a disgusting idea. Then, I came up with another idea while walking through the airport in San Antonio.

As everyone knows, everything in Texas is oversized, from its land mass to the hearts of its people. Well, in the airport, I found enormous Texas-sized jelly beans on display on some counter.

What a colorful—dare I say it? even tempting—way to demonstrate the sifting of solids without being too graphic! Viewers would definitely get the connection and wouldn't have to look at candy that resembled poop.

It scares me sometimes what goes through my mind at any given time. Who'd have thought that oversized jelly beans in the San Antonio airport would be the perfect answer for a kitty litter box demonstration? But we tried it—and it worked!

Electronic retailing is powerful in two different ways. There's the visual power, which we've just discussed, and then there's the economic power. You have to be prepared for the power of electronic retailing. It can chew you up and spit you out before you know it, or it can be the entrepreneur's winning lottery ticket.

A word about being unprepared: A substitute on-air guest showed up for a product speaking broken English. If that wasn't bad enough, he was also soft-spoken and monotone.

I personally like on-air guests who have accents—they tend to add charm and credibility. But, the combination of being soft-spoken along with broken English made the presentation hard to listen to.

You know what that means! The passive listener never became an active listener.

By following the guidelines in the following chapter about how to present your product on QVC, you'll hopefully be among those sharing in the entrepreneur's lottery.

Chapter Nine

How to Get on QVC

My life changed as the result of a product that I believed in. This product changed my life personally and financially. Do you have a product concept? Do you have the next better mousetrap? If you do, this chapter will help you get into QVC and the world of electronic retailing. Remember, I am NOT an employee of QVC. I'm an outside marketing consultant and the products' creators are my clients. But my success with Lite Bites and, let's face it, the fact that my dad founded the company, has given me a special place there (although not a special place to park!). By now I know almost everyone who works there. I appear on-air and promote a very heavily reordered and successful product. I also suggest products to QVC's buyers for possible on-air presentation through my consulting business, Segel Associates. In this chapter, I'll describe some of the other products I've represented so that you can get an idea of what QVC looks for in a product that should sell successfully on-air.

During the time I've been associated with QVC, I've learned a few things that just might help you appreciate the work and dedication that goes into each and every presentation you see on TV. And, as an added bonus, what I observe about QVC just might help you bring your product to a buyer's attention and a possible on-air presentation. That on-air appearance might just change your life. My first on-air appearance certainly did!

I've heard QVC described as controlled chaos. I don't think this controlled chaos is unique to QVC, rather it's the way many of us operate in business nowadays. Why? Because we are on information overload.

At most other businesses, they at least close shop once in a while. QVC never closes. There's no nine to five. The show goes on live 24 hours a day, seven days a week. The faxes, phone calls, e-mails, and paperwork never stop. It is crucial that you keep this in mind when you're dealing with QVC's merchandising department as a prospective vendor. Be mindful of the buyer's tight schedule when communicating with QVC.

Before contacting a QVC buyer, however, you should first obtain all the available information about QVC and becoming a QVC vendor. There are two Web sites that are invaluable for this purpose—QVC's home page at www.qvc.com, where you can learn a great deal about current products, and www.vendor.studiopark.com, which contains a section specifically for prospective vendors.

You'll then need to obtain Product Submittal forms. You can do this either by calling Vendor Relations at 888-NEW-ITEM (639-4836) or through the Web at www.vendor.studiopark.com where you'll click on "How to Become a QVC Vendor." Here you can fill out and submit the forms on-line along with a digital image file of your product. If you don't have a digital file, you can still fill out the forms, print them out, and send them by s-mail, along with a brochure or photo of your product. Mailing instructions are included on the site.

Wait at least three weeks after receipt of product submittal before you follow up. Keep in mind that there is a fine line between good follow-up and being a pain in the neck. I don't think any of us has ever been taught the proper way to leave a voice-mail message, or send an e-mail or a fax, so let me take a moment and tell you the basics. These points will help you in dealing with QVC and with others in your personal and professional life.

When sending an e-mail, if you type in all caps it is interpreted as yelling. When leaving a voice-mail message, you don't need to tell your life story, nor should you leave more than one message on the same subject during the same day.

When you call too many times, it is very easy for the buyer to hit the delete button and tune you out. To the buyer, you're like the boy who cried wolf.

If you've called the same buyer three or four times the same day, with basically the same message, but the fourth message had a very important question, I would bet you that the fourth message would be deleted before the buyer hears the first few seconds of the message.

Now let's talk about the proper way to send a fax to a company as large, as busy, and as widespread as QVC. In my home office, for example, the fax machine sits right next to my desk. No chance of anything getting misplaced or lost. But at a place like QVC, the fax would never be delivered to its intended recipient unless it contained, at the least, a cover sheet and the number of pages the fax included. You see, QVC has over six thousand employees, divided up into many "neighborhoods" (the planners, the guests, the buyers, the producers, the executives, etc.). All these people share lots of equipment in multiples areas of a large, two-story building. It's an overwhelming sight until you know it.

At QVC, a single fax machine may be shared by a number of departments and many people. Therefore, here are some tips on making sure your faxes get through:
- Always include a cover page.
- Note the number of pages, including the cover page.
- Include the recipient's name and voice phone number.
- Finally, leave a voice-mail message letting your buyer know that you sent a fax, the number of the pages, and the time you sent it.

If you have a product that makes sense for QVC and intend to make a presentation to a QVC buyer, please keep this in mind: QVC buyers and planners are under constant time pressure from an overload of submissions. For the typical QVC buyer, life is a never-ending cycle of pressure.

Here are some facts about a buyer's life at QVC:
- More than 65 phone calls per day.
- More than 55 voice mails.
- More than 40 e-mails.

This means that the typical buyer is being asked to make 160 responses per day. All that before he or she can even talk to you in any detail about your prospective product.

So, how do the buyers get their jobs done? They are very dedicated, efficient, and hardworking.

It's a hectic new world out there. QVC is where you get a real sense of American commerce today. Sometimes it seems that everybody in the world is trying to get into QVC. For that reason, QVC has over 120 buyers whose job it is to sift through submitted products and also to source new products through various trade shows. So, if you're a retail buyer, QVC is a great place to work.

In an average year, QVC's buyers send 25,000 new products to QVC's Quality Assurance Lab. Just imagine how many products they had to look at before they got down to 25,000!

Keeping all these facts in mind, you might think that you don't have a chance of getting a buyer to return a phone call. But remember, a QVC buyer is still a buyer. His or her job is to find product. By doing it right, having a good product and complete presentations, and being respectful of the buyer's time, you can get in the door and get on the air.

Yes, we all know that time never stops, but that's especially true at QVC. In a typical department store, your product is on the shelf and it just sits there. It is subject primarily to limitations of shelf space, not usually to limitations of time (unless it's a seasonal product, like handcrafted Christmas tree ornaments).

At QVC, retailing is primarily about time because QVC is on 24 hours a day, seven days a week and dead air, as we all know, is unacceptable. The cliché "time is money" is doubly true at QVC.

At QVC there is never time to catch up. As soon as one show is over, the next show is around the corner. Imagine a sitcom, or a movie, changing sets, actors, and producers every 15 minutes or so, with no break in between. This phenomenon, indigenous to electronic retailing, even applies if you're fortunate enough—as I have been—to be tapped as an on-air guest for Today's Special Value. That means that you'll be making on-air presentations five to seven times during one 24-hour period. One day you're setting million-dollar sales records; the very next day, it's someone else's turn. You're history. The next Today's Special Value product and guest are on deck. QVC viewers may have just bought thousands of boxes of Lite Bites, but now it is time for the next herringbone necklace to hit the stage. While the phones are ringing off the hook for the necklace, you are schlepping your bags out the door as yesterday's news.

This phenomenon becomes even more interesting when I arrive home and the next day is trash day. I'm now also carrying out the trash.

From personal experience, I can tell you it's a strange feeling to be an on-air personality one day and carrying out the trash the next.

The point is that if you have a product you wish to present to QVC, be mindful of the time pressures that the men and the women are under who do the buying and the planning.

—

Sitting in the cafeteria at QVC, where most of my internal business meetings take place, I have overheard many presentations for new products. So many times I've wanted to jump to my feet and go over to the meeting and say, "May I help you?" because, based on my on-air and marketing experiences, I know I could.

I hear so many miscues on the part of some vendors. Knowing how definitive the answers have to be at QVC, I'm always surprised at how unprepared many would-be vendors are about even the most basic information.

For instance, I have heard buyers at QVC ask, "How much can I buy this for if I buy three thousand pieces?" All too often, the vendor is stumped for an answer.

Other questions buyers may ask are:
- How many of these can you make per month?
- How can you substantiate that claim?
- Has the product been tested?

My intention is to point you in the right direction at QVC.

As the world's largest electronic retailer, QVC gets swamped by prospective vendors from around the world. In the course of a typical month, QVC buyers receive inquiries from more than 10,000 people with dreams. Of those 10,000, only 1% get on-air. That's right: 1% get on-air.

But don't let this fact intimidate you, because I'm here to show you how to improve your odds. Although Lite Bites is the only product I represent on-air, through my consulting business, I advise people about the best ways to position their products for possible on-air presentation. When I see a good idea that will work on-air, I sometimes arrange to represent its proprietor in his or her efforts to break in at QVC. If you watch QVC, you probably are familiar with some of the products I represent, such as Tahitian black pearls and the LitterQuick cat litter boxes you read about earlier. I've also represented Fluttering Wonders, which were invented by the guys who invented the Lava Lamps that were popular in the 1970s. Fluttering Wonders are sticks that you insert into your houseplants. At the top end of the stick is something that looks like a butterfly flapping its wings. The effect of the sticks with the butterflies on them is that there is motion constantly around your plants. It's a neat idea, aesthetically pleasing, and it demonstrates well on television.

I also represent Biko, the only bicycle seat to be patented since the invention of bike seats. Its unique feature is its dropped horn that relieves pressure on a certain part of your anatomy when you sit on a bike seat. Any of you who have taken long bike tours or simply like to ride a bike for exercise know exactly the kind of pressure I mean. Richard

Hobson developed Biko and he's set to go on QVC. Again, this is a product that demonstrates well on-air, its concept is easy to grasp, and it has a connected spokesperson. It also satisfies the "problem/solution" requirement quite nicely — what do you do about those very uncomfortable bike seats? I expect this product will do very well.

Another product I'm developing for presentation on QVC comes from a guy named Harry Kuperschmidt. It's called Freezy. The problem that Freezy solves is something that dog owners face every day, sometimes several times a day: how to pick up dog poop gracefully and with the least amount of mess. If you're a dog owner in certain parts of the country, you are *required* to clean up after your dog. Until now, it's been a messy job, one the owner has to do with plastic bags, or newspapers, or disposable gloves. Freezy is a propellant that, when sprayed on the poop, turns to ice, thereby making the messy stuff much easier to gather up and throw away. Now, obviously, we have the same problem in demonstrating this product on-air that we had with Fresh Magic kitty litter. How do you show how beautifully this product works without grossing people out, especially when it's presented on the Morning Show? Well, again, my brain started to click and I came up with the perfect solution: You present a video of Harry approaching dog owners in Manhattan's Central Park and ask them to try it—and you videotape their pleased reactions to using it—and not the actual duty itself. Voila! Since this stuff really works, the dog owners provide the "problem/solution" image that will sell this product. By the way, this product is for any dog owner and can be kept on hand when Fido has an accident in the house. It really makes clean-up a lot easier! This product is still being tested by QVC's Quality Assurance

Department, but I am confident it will pass and it will probably do well on the air.

Perhaps now you can see the way my mind works. I've developed a program for on-air presentation—what works and what doesn't—and I'm sharing its high points with you now.

Keep in mind that for your product to get on-air, you have to replace something that is currently being presented. It's competitive and not unlike the battle for shelf space in your local supermarket.

Or, to use another example, the situation resembles rookie football camp. Only so many players can make the cut, and you always have the new kid on the block who's ready to replace the veteran. From QVC's point of view, this kind of competition is healthy and results in only the finest products making it in front of the camera. In the end, it is the viewers who decide which products stay and which products go.

What do I mean by the finest products?

Typically, what really works at QVC, as I think I have demonstrated, is a great product, with a great story, and a connected spokesperson who can interact with the product on the air. It's that difficult, and it's that simple. The point is, if you have a great product that solves a problem that a lot of viewers share, then getting into QVC is not hard. You just have to understand and anticipate QVC's needs.

Here's how it all begins:

Since I am a product rep who positions products for electronic retailing, the process starts with me the way it starts with most of QVC's 120 buyers. I receive a phone call and the caller says, "I have a product I'd like to get on QVC."

I say, "Great! Can you ship it to me?"

The usual response is, "No, we're still in the conceptual stage."

I prefer that products be as close to a final stage as possible. If it is a pre-production sample, I always request that the sample be as close as possible to what QVC viewers will be receiving in their homes.

I'm not saying QVC will not consider products that are still in the idea stage. It's just that it's a lot harder to answer many of the needed questions when the product is not completed.

For me, if the product is in a conceptual stage, that is a problem and will show up on a list of do's and don'ts we'll be discussing.

Assuming that the prospects have a product that they can ship to me, I then ask why they think their product is better than a similar product on QVC. This is my own version of a David Letterman–type top ten list.

In other words, I ask for ten key selling benefits (that can be substantiated; more on this later) that will be part of your on-air presentation. Some of these benefits may be on-air demonstrations that you feel are good enough to knock something else off the air. Of those ten virtues, you generally will not use more than three during an 8- to 12-minute presentation.

Okay, now I've got two product samples (one for the buyer and one for QVC's Quality Assurance Department) and the key selling benefits. So we're on our way to preparing a presentation for the buyer.

What does that presentation look like? Remembering that the clock never stops at QVC, and that the buyers are extremely busy, make sure that your presentation is to the point and that you have anticipated questions and have definitive answers.

Here's what the opening page of your three-page presentation should look like:

OPENING PAGE

1. THE PRODUCT

Describe what makes your product unique and why you feel QVC would benefit from having this product on-air. QVC's own home page, www.qvc.com, is a great source for product information. Use the search capabilities to look for a product category similar to yours. You will then be able to position your product by explaining how or why it is unique.

2. THE GUEST

If you have watched QVC—which you should do to grasp the fundamentals—you surely have noticed that it takes two to make a presentation, the QVC host and the guest, the guest being the individual who directly represents and presents the product. (The "guest" is QVC's word for the on-air spokesperson.)

As the guest, try to give QVC as much background as possible about your connection to the product. For example, did you invent the product, test it, or benefit from its use?

You should be able to tell a story about your involvement with the product. The host gives the facts; you, the guest, tell the story behind those facts in the most compelling way possible.

That's the power of QVC and electronic retailing that is different from traditional retailing: The product has a voice and a story. In a department store, your product sits on a shelf with, one hopes, appealing packaging. But on the shelf it doesn't have either a voice or a story.

3. THE PRICE

Keeping in mind that the V in QVC stands for value, make sure that you are truly giving value to QVC and QVC's 60

million-plus viewers. Based on QVC's buying power, in
my opinion, QVC's on-air price should at least be equal to
regular retail pricing or, preferably, less. That is value!
Also remember that QVC can never go down in price.
Why? Don't you see red when a product you bought last
week is marked down this week? Sure, most stores will
honor the lower price, but you've got to remember to find
the sales slip, bring it in, and ask for it. QVC's policy is
never to disappoint or inconvenience a customer like that.
Therefore, you must keep in mind that the price you've
established will remain constant and will be as good as it
gets.

4. LEAD TIME and SHELF LIFE

State the actual, realistic lead time you require to manufac-
ture your product.

How much product are we talking about? Typically,
$20,000 to $30,000 at QVC retail for your first order. How
did I come up with this number? Keeping in mind that
QVC's sales are over $2 billion a year, and that there are
524,160 minutes in QVC's year, you come up with an average of about $3,300 a minute. Multiply that figure by the
eight minutes you'll typically spend on-air. If your product
is very expensive or inexpensive, the numbers may get
skewed. But QVC looks for products that can sell in that
range with their first on-air presentation.

Based on an average presentation your sales should come
close to a sellout. There are many variables, but this is the
target.

Moreover, let QVC know the shelf life of your product
and any specific storage requirements. In most cases, it is
necessary for QVC to have all goods in its warehouse at

least two weeks prior to your on-air date. Keep that in mind when estimating your lead times.

When trying to answer the lead-time question, you may need to know the quantity of items QVC intends to buy. Assuming that your item would not be positioned as a special promotional item, such as a Today's Special Value, QVC could order anywhere from $20,000 to $30,000 worth of product at QVC retail as a first order.

There are a number of variables that can affect this first order:
- Is there a guest?
- Is this a premiere?
- Is this a new category?
- Does this kind of product have a track record on QVC?

Since there are so many variables, make sure you understand what QVC expects from your first order. I've mentioned that QVC expects your product to be in its warehouse two weeks prior to any show date. However, for your first show, I generally recommend that you give yourself a little more lead time, just to be safe.

5. THE PACKAGE

QVC has its own Quality Assurance Department—you can be sure that your product will be tested for its function. It will also be dropped up to 11 times on all sides and seams to see that it doesn't break in its box. QVC has 120 engineers who test and retest every product before it goes on-air. They test over and above the letter of the law. Why? Quality is QVC's FIRST name! If it isn't high quality, it can and will be returned by the customer, and that isn't good for the company's image or its bottom line. Remember: 35% of the products that pass the buyers pass the Quality Assurance Department on the first try. Another 40% pass after the vendor has made adjustments that the QA people recommend. And 25% of the products submitted never pass and are ultimately rejected. If you have come this far with your product, be absolutely sure that it lives up to QVC's rigorous quality standards.

6. POSSIBLE POSITIONING

There are numerous opportunities to showcase your product, including many themed one-hour shows, such as *The Morning Show, Jewelry Showcase, QVC Sampler, In the Kitchen with Bob, The Family Room, Picture Perfect, High-Tech Toys and Electronics, Cleaning Solutions,* and many others. Chances are you are an avid QVC viewer and know exactly what theme your product falls under. In this part of your presentation, you might suggest what type of show will best benefit your product. Keep in mind that you do not control the airtime. QVC does. This is why you should suggest and not insist. For example, the LitterQuick Litter Box System might be best positioned in a show titled "Problem Solvers." Or, a product that makes you feel or look more attractive might do well in a show titled "Beauty Solutions."

Those are the six points to be covered in the crucial page one of your presentation to the QVC buyer.

PAGE TWO

Here's where you point out your ten key selling benefits. Keep in mind the difference between a feature and a benefit. Remember the discussion we had back in my real estate days about the Pond & Spitz brochure that listed benefits and features of a particular house? A feature might be that the ceramic tile in the kitchen was installed in wet bed cement, and the benefit to the home buyer might be superior installation with fewer maintenance problems. Another example: A house might have three full baths—that's a feature. The benefit to the home owner is added convenience and privacy for large families and their guests.

In my job as a representative of potential QVC items, I'll cite as an example what I call the biscotti case regarding features and benefits. When I spoke to the manufacturer, the woman told me that her company used the "finest chocolate from around the world."

To me, that was a feature, not a benefit.

I said, "That's terrific, but what does that mean to the QVC viewer?"

Her response was, "It's the best-tasting chocolate."

"Aha," I said. "Now that's the benefit, and that's what you need to say."

In this part of your presentation, be sure you list ten benefits, not features, and make sure you can substantiate all of them. You'll probably have time on-air to discuss only two or three of the ten benefits, but, as you've heard me say what I learned from my father, it never hurts to overprepare your presentation. You are a more powerful and persuasive spokesperson if you do.

It is crucial that you be in a position to substantiate your claims. Be careful how you word your presentation. Let me caution you against claiming your product "will" do something, because it is virtually impossible to guarantee that a product will do anything, given the diverse nature of the people who might buy it. Your phrasing needs to be that your product "should" or "may" bring about the intended result.

Saying your product "will" do something leaves you open to the prospect of your product's being unable to fulfill its promise to everyone, which can translate into a high return rate.

This listing of your product's benefits completes page two of your presentation to the buyer.

To help you better understand what a presentation should look like, the following couple of pages are examples of blue cards. Blue cards are the cards that are used by the show hosts to highlight key product benefits and the order of the show. (See sample blue cards on pages 164–165.)

Why are the cards blue? I have no idea.

PAGE THREE

Page three begins with your basic vendor information. This should include such details as your mailing address, phone numbers, and key contact persons. Additionally, include where purchase orders should be sent, where you ship from, and, if returns are coming back to you, where they should be shipped.

This page completes your three-page presentation that you bring with you when you meet your QVC buyer for the first time. I suggest you bring with you at least four sets of this presentation: two for the buyer, one for Quality Assurance, and one for you.

Now that you have an understanding of QVC's needs, and know what a good package should look like, you are ready to submit it to QVC's Vendor Relations Department. If they like what they see, they'll contact you to set up a meeting with a buyer.

If you are one of the lucky ones to get that call, you'll want to be as prepared as you possibly can be for the meeting. Review your material once again and try to anticipate any questions the buyer might ask. QVC is better informed to make quick decisions on your product when your meeting is well planned and you have all the questions answered even before they are asked. A well-prepared presentation is no guarantee of getting you in the door, but it will give you an edge against your competition.

—

Before proceeding, let's remember that QVC is a moving target. It can, and does, respond instantly to current events and trends in the marketplace. This triggerlike response can sometimes give the people who work there and you, the suppliers, gray hairs because everyone has to be able to adjust swiftly. At the same time, it can be very rewarding.

A current event, say something in the way of a sports, weather, or news-related item, could make your product exactly what the QVC viewer needs at the moment. For example, the start of winter weather or a major snowstorm is a perfect opportunity for unique snow shovels or products that make it easier to walk on ice. Obviously the Arctic 180 ear warmers do well during this time of year.

A dramatic example of how quickly QVC moves involves baseball. Minutes after Mark McGuire hit his sixty-second home run, QVC interrupted its regular live program with a live collectibles program featuring replicas of that home-run ball personally signed by McGuire. In the end, more than $2 million in sales were chalked up in about an hour.

So keep this tip handy: When you get that appointment at QVC, be sure the buyer knows that you can respond at a moment's notice.

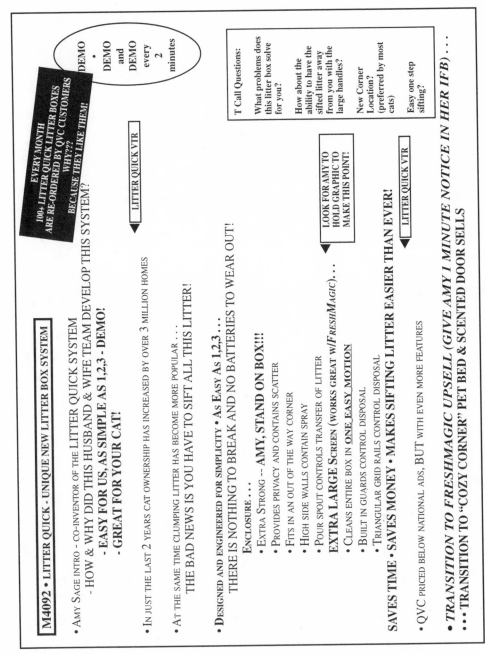

M4092 • LITTER QUICK - UNIQUE NEW LITTER BOX SYSTEM

• AMY SAGE INTRO - CO-INVENTOR OF THE LITTER QUICK SYSTEM
 - HOW & WHY DID THIS HUSBAND & WIFE TEAM DEVELOP THIS SYSTEM?
  - **EASY FOR US, AS SIMPLE AS 1,2,3 - DEMO!**
   - **GREAT FOR YOUR CAT!**

• IN JUST THE LAST 2 YEARS CAT OWNERSHIP HAS INCREASED BY OVER 3 MILLION HOMES

• AT THE SAME TIME CLUMPING LITTER HAS BECOME MORE POPULAR . . . .
  THE BAD NEWS IS YOU HAVE TO SIFT ALL THIS LITTER!

• **DESIGNED AND ENGINEERED FOR SIMPLICITY • AS EASY AS 1,2,3 . . .**
  THERE IS NOTHING TO BREAK AND NO BATTERIES TO WEAR OUT!
   ENCLOSURE . . . .
    • EXTRA STRONG -- **AMY, STAND ON BOX!!!**
    • PROVIDES PRIVACY AND CONTAINS SCATTER
    • FITS IN AN OUT OF THE WAY CORNER
    • HIGH SIDE WALLS CONTAIN SPRAY
    • POUR SPOUT CONTROLS TRANSFER OF LITTER
   EXTRA LARGE SCREEN (WORKS GREAT W/*FRESHMAGIC*) . . .
    • CLEANS ENTIRE BOX IN **ONE EASY MOTION**
    • BUILT IN GUARDS CONTROL DISPOSAL
    • TRIANGULAR GRID RAILS CONTROL DISPOSAL
  SAVES TIME • SAVES MONEY • MAKES SIFTING LITTER EASIER THAN EVER!

• QVC PRICED BELOW NATIONAL ADS, BUT WITH EVEN MORE FEATURES

• *TRANSITION TO FRESHMAGIC UPSELL (GIVE AMY 1 MINUTE NOTICE IN HER IFB) . . . .*
• *. . . TRANSITION TO "COZY CORNER" PET BED & SCENTED DOOR SELLS*

EVERY MONTH
100+ LITTER QUICK LITTER BOXES
ARE RE-ORDERED BY QVC CUSTOMERS
WHY???
BECAUSE THEY LIKE THEM!

▶ LITTER QUICK VTR

DEMO
•
DEMO
and
DEMO
every
2
minutes

LOOK FOR AMY TO
HOLD GRAPHIC TO
MAKE THIS POINT!

▶ LITTER QUICK VTR

T Call Questions:

What problems does
this litter box solve
for you?

How about the
ability to have the
sifted litter away
from you with the
large handles?

New Corner
Location?
(preferred by most
cats)

Easy one step
sifting?

Blue card sample

M5321 • LITTER QUICK - COZY CORNET PET BED

• PREMIERING TODAY ! ! !

   - THE QVC VIEWER KNOWS THAT CATS LOVE CORNERS, THATS WHY THEY LOVE LITTER QUICK

     - COZY CRONER FITS IN ANY CORNER

• DESIGNED BY CAT OWNERS FOR CAT OWNERS . . .

     - TRIANGLE DESIGNS MIRRORS LITTER QUICK'S CORNER DESIGN

- SIZED TO FIT RIGHT ON TOP OF THE LITTER QUICK LITTER BOX - THE CUSTOMERS ASKED FOR THIS DESIGN!!!

> **GREAT POINT**

   - THE REMOVABLE PILLOW IS ALSO REVERSABLE

     - WARM FUR SIDE

     - COOL COTTON SIDE

> **GREAT POINT**

- BOTH THE COVER AND THE PILLOW ARE MACHINE WASHABLE

- NONSKID BOTTOM ALLOWS THE COZY CORNER PET BED TO BE PLACED ANYWHERE. . . .

     - ON TOP THE THE LITTER QUICK BOX

     - OR ANY OTHER SMOOTH SURFACE THAT YOUR CAT MAY PREFER

EVERY MONTH
100+ LITTER QUICK LITTER BOXES
ARE RE-ORDERED BY QVC CUSTOMERS
WHY???
BECAUSE THEY LIKE THEM!

DEMO
•
DEMO
and
DEMO
every
MINUTE

T Call Questions:

What problems does this litter box solve for you?

How about the ability to have the sifted litter away from you with the large handles?

New Corner Location? (preferred by most cats)

Easy one step sifting?

Blue card sample

165

166 • MAKING IT AT QVC

"Yes" is Great, but "No" is also Okay at QVC—
Dealing with Rejection

How many times in life have you gone after something and found yourself facing rejection? "NO!" was the answer. What did you do? Slither away in defeat? Or did you fight back? Most likely you fought back and did so by repositioning yourself. You asked for a raise late one afternoon and found out later that your boss's most receptive time is first thing in the morning. (I've found that mornings are the best times to deal with complex issues.)

Remember, in the world of commerce, as in all areas of life, you are a product. Whether you know it or not, you're always selling yourself. At work or at home, among coworkers, family, and friends, you always want to be at your best.

Yes, you are a product to your spouse, to your friends, and to your boss. That may sound cold, but think about it. When you get married, you reposition your value. Your dependency on each other may change. You share the caring of your home and you need to care for each other.

Then, when your life seems in balance, you have a child. You are definitely repositioning your value when you have a child.

What are you worth to your boss? You're a product here, too. When you ask for a raise, you are trying to reestablish your value. Your boss will be measuring or re-measuring your value, just as he or she would any other product.

You're always positioning yourself, and when your first approach doesn't work, you try another approach. Kids are great at repositioning when they're told no. How many times have your kids been told no but then got a "yes" after they restated the question over and over again?

They wanted that extra piece of chocolate and finally won you over when they asked if they could save it for later. You relented because the question was asked in a different way. (Probably, they just wore you down.)

You can't make people do what they don't want to do, but you can give them reasons to motivate themselves so that they eventually do what you want them to do. By using different approaches you can turn a negative into a positive.

The best example I know of how this kind of persistence pays off is that of the now-legendary Pat Croce, who wanted to buy the Philadelphia 76ers, at the time a terrific basketball team, from then-owner Harold Katz. At the time, Croce was not well known. He was a physical therapist and trainer. He owned a couple of gyms. But he regularly phoned Katz and asked if the team was for sale. He always took Katz's "no" to mean, "not now, call back later." And Croce did. Every couple of months, Pat would call Harold until one day, Harold said, "Well, maybe not yet" instead of his usual "no." Pat took that to mean that Harold was ready to talk and invited him to lunch. Eventually his persistence paid off, because eventually he did buy the team. Once he determined that Katz was changing his mind, he went to Comcast, put together a financial package, and accomplished his dream. I asked him to speak at one of our Builder's League meetings because he's a great guy and a terrific motivator. He told us this story of how he bought his dream team. If he'd taken "no" for an answer, where would he be today?

How does this story relate to getting your product on QVC? One thing I've learned is to plant a seed in the other person's mind so that your idea becomes his or her idea.

That's what we marketing types call positioning.

Now, if your product gets the heave-ho from Vendor Relations, try to find out why. Lite Bites was originally rejected by QVC. Yes, the founder's son was turned down. In the case of Lite Bites, the product evidently did not fit a certain department's product mix. I had presented it to the Health and Fitness buyer, thinking that was the most appropriate spot for it. What I didn't know was that they weren't taking on ingestible diet products at that time. So what did I do? I found another department within QVC that would take it—the Health and Beauty Department. Sometimes repositioning is just that simple. The product is right, but you're showing it to the wrong people. Knowing which door to knock on is also part of positioning and repositioning.

You also have to be creative—think outside the box. It's not just a question of which door to knock on. You might pair or associate your product with another product and thereby open a door you could not open before. We did just that with a no-fat pizza product that some fellows brought to me. Now, I've gone on record saying that no-fat is not great for you, because those products substitute salt or sugar for the fat to make the product taste good and we tend to eat more because we think no-fat is good for us. So I was able to get the creators, Fitness Quest, to turn the concept into something slightly different: a low-fat pizza that we're marketing as a health product. We got them to change the recipe a bit, so that the crust is made with oat bran. (Oat bran has lots of nutritional benefits plus a bit of fat in it.) I also paired it with another product that might not have sold on-air on its own, Cardia® Salt, from AMBI Inc. Cardia is a reduced-sodium salt that tastes just like regular salt but contains less than half the sodium. Its health benefits have been confirmed with some very impressive clinical research studies. I now use Cardia Salt all the time at home. On-air, we'll talk about the healthy, low-fat pizzas, which come flash-frozen and packaged in dry ice, six to a box, and, inside the package, we'll include a sample shaker of Cardia Salt, with instructions about how to reorder just the salt (and the pizzas, too, of course) if the customer likes the product. That way, people can taste how good the pizzas are, how good the salt is, and reorder if they want. And Cardia Salt gets a marketing boost it might not otherwise have had.

When I first decided to represent Lite Bites, I had to find the right department in which to present it. The second time I approached QVC, I found a very receptive assistant buyer by the name of Jeanine Gendrachi. Jeanine has become a full buyer and has been a great asset to the growth of Lite Bites at QVC, under the direction of Judy Grishaver.

So, one option of product repositioning is finding the right department. In many cases you won't have a choice. Some products are too specific to fit into a variety of departments. If you've submitted a treadmill to QVC and it was rejected, you can't reposition it in the collectibles department by saying it's a limited edition. But take a product like a dietary supplement for your pet. Does it go into the Pet Department or the Health Department? Incidentally, we've found at QVC that pet vitamins don't sell well, because it's hard to tell whether the pet is actually benefiting from a vitamin. I mean, the dog can't tell you how much better he's feeling after ingesting a vitamin. But if you tweak the idea a bit, and offer a pet joint-support dietary supplement, then it is possible to demonstrate that an aging pet is actually getting better, walking with more spring in his step—and those products should sell well.

Product positioning is a very important step in getting any product to the customer, whether electronically or in any retail medium. Now, what do you do if QVC says this product of yours doesn't fit?

Talk to the buyer and ask why. That's your first recourse.

• Is it a quality issue?
• Is it a pricing issue?
• Is the timing wrong?
• Is it right for electronic retailing?

You can't overcome the objections until you know what they are.

My recommendation is to drop back ten yards and punt. Take your product back and rethink it. Be cooperative with QVC and don't burn any bridges. Sure you're disappointed that the product didn't fly, but don't give up hope! Remember Pat Croce's example. Here are some things to consider:

• You can repackage it.
• You can rename it.
• You can reconfigure it.

You'd be surprised how one small change can make all the difference. Sometimes just adding a phrase to a product can turn failure into success.

No better example of that is my personal experience with Lite Bites Daily Advantage Vitamin. This product was first introduced as a stand-alone vitamin and did poorly on-air. Obviously, the typical QVC viewer thought, 'We love Marv for helping us fight fat. But we do not understand why we should buy a vitamin from him.'

Here's where some serious repositioning comes in. I had only a few hours that particular day before the next appearance of the vitamin. When we went back on-air with it, we showed it with the Lite Bite bars—an icon product on QVC. By presenting the vitamin on-air a second time as "a vitamin you may want to take while losing weight," we were able to double the sales from the first appearance.

Later that same day, we tripled what we doubled. And we did all this by connecting the vitamin to an established brand. The key here was not only repositioning, but timing. In electronic retailing, you're dealing not in days, weeks, or months, but in minutes; at most, in hours. You learn to think quickly on your feet.

Being an on-air guest on QVC is like doing improv. As for Lite Bites, I only had a few hours to reposition this product and I did so as a vitamin you may want to use while losing weight. This repositioning involved not only changing my on-air presentation, but it also meant reshooting the still image of the vitamin bottle. Here's where my work as Franklin Mint's photographer-mole paid off. (Who could have known?) This new image had a box of Lite Bites bars out of focus in the background behind the vitamins. Therefore we offered the viewer an association of the new product with the tried-and-true best-selling product. And it worked!

Such quick responsiveness is something you'd never be able to do in traditional retailing.

Carolyn Hendrickson in the Vendor Relations Department at QVC told me about a certain "healthy" walking shoe that is selling well through the Shoe Department, but could have just as easily gone into the Health Department. The reason QVC put it in the Shoe Department has more to do with QVC than with the product: The Shoe Department is better equipped to fulfill orders that come in for various sizes than the Health Department; therefore, it's cost effective to put the shoe in the Shoe Department, where it's doing just fine.

I'm working with a product now that needs to be reposi- tioned. It's a plant growth-enhancing product made from liquified peat moss that works beautifully. I've revived near- ly dead plants with it. I even put it in a pond near my house and it reduced the algae problem I was having. Unfortunately the on-air spokesperson wasn't as effective as he might have been. He developed the product, and so fit QVC's requirement of a spokesperson connected with the product, but he's a scientist and his presentation was a bit dry. He didn't really connect with the viewers. What I would like to do is rename the product and attach a well- known plant expert to it, who can talk about the product's benefits in a much more convincing and passionate way.

Remember, QVC knows its customers. Based on its years of experience, QVC knows what will succeed on-air and what won't. Therefore, once your product has been approved, you'd be wise to heed QVC's advice on the best way to present your product line. Otherwise, you're setting yourself up for failure.

I'll give you an example. A nationally known doctor wanted to come on QVC with his company's health-related products—and QVC was eager to have him. QVC wanted him to come on with a series of videotapes that were suc- cessfully sold on national TV. His company, however, insist- ed that he come on-air with a different product, an ingestible. The outcome was that his ingestible product did not sell well on the air and ended up with those dreaded ini- tials emblazoned on its shipping cartons: RTV—return to vendor.

I would call this company's decision to put the ingestible on the air counterpositioning. The company didn't listen to QVC's advice or benefit from its expertise in electronic retailing. From QVC's point of view, the ingestible was similar to a product that was already a smash hit on QVC. It was therefore coming up against an established brand. QVC's idea was to establish this famous doctor on QVC with the tried-and true videos, then branch out into other products once QVC viewers trusted him.

Our famous doctor and his company learned their lesson. They are now developing new products for QVC that will be unique to him. He's learned repositioning the hard way. Almost a year later, after QVC returned two of his original products, the doctor is finally bringing his videos to QVC and, if successful, will sell other products as well.

Another example of not taking "no" for an answer comes from one of my best friends at QVC, Joy Mangano. You remember her from earlier in this book—she developed the Miracle Mop. We described earlier that when the mop first went on-air without her, it did not do well, and the remaining inventory was going to be returned.

Joy was faced with the dreaded "no." End of story, right? Not quite.

How did she turn "no" into "yes"? She first asked her buyer what the problem was, then asked if she could go on-air with the product and demonstrate it herself and tell the story of how she invented it. More than ten million Miracle Mops later, we know how successful that repositioning turned out to be.

The mop was the same great product, but Joy knew it needed the connected spokesperson to make the difference. The same story told by the connected, passionate spokesperson was the key.

What better example is there of what I mean when I say that you, the individual, are a product! Even in the initial stages of preparing your papers for the QVC buyer, think of all the questions that buyer might have about your product and be prepared to answer them. If you still get a "no," find out WHY and go back to the drawing board. If you believe in your product, you just might succeed and be that 1% who gets his or her day in court, or, more appropriately, gets that first ten-minute time slot on-air.

Going On-Air for the First Time

What's it like going on-air at QVC the first time? Well, it's a little like your first sexual experience: Hours of anticipation, and it's all over in a few minutes—and you're not sure how good your performance was.

When I relayed this observation to a buyer at QVC, she added the following, giving it the female spin: "And it's rare that you get a return phone call."

I know it's a cliché, but this much is true at QVC—keep it short and sweet. In all my years of sales training, I've heard many experts say that people start to tune you out if you talk for more than ten minutes.

A famous new-home sales trainer says new-home sales presentations should be limited to ten minutes. He calls this the Ten-Minute Drill. Donald Trump himself, the master of the business game, says no business meeting should go beyond 15 minutes. Why? He gets bored.

The point is, within ten minutes you should be able to convey all the benefits of your product. Let me underscore this message. Within ten minutes you should be able to introduce yourself and properly present your product's key benefits and selling points. Is it any wonder, then, that QVC typically allows 8 to 12 minutes for an on-air guest presentation?

Remember, I never expected to be on-air with Lite Bites, or with anything. Never thought of myself as an on-air kind of guy, except for this: I'm always open to new challenges. I guess you'd call that the entrepreneurial spirit. This country is all about finding something good, something new, and going with it all the way. Or, finding something that's already being done—but doing it better. As a matter of fact, that very adventuresome call of the wild inspired my dad to create both the Franklin Mint and QVC. I like to believe it was this spirit that he passed on to me.

When I met the buyer at QVC to present my personal endorsement of Lite Bites, I expected to be used as an off-air pre-taped testimonial. Nothing more.

So I nearly fell off the chair when the buyer said quite nonchalantly, "You'll go on-air with the product."

I said, "What? I've never been on-air before."

She said, "You'll do fine. You're a natural."

That was good to hear, but even a "natural" needs training, which I'd never had. What I did have was this: a great product. As I've said, what works on QVC is a great story with a great product—not a pushy sales pitch.

But I was beset by three concerns. First, not fainting on-air. Second, doing justice to a product that I believed in. Third, and perhaps my main concern, being better than anyone else since I was Joe Segel's son and, as I know from all my past experience, I'd be held to a higher standard. At least that's what I always believed, and frankly, it's something that's motivated me throughout my life. Such motivation—the feeling that you're always being watched and judged—has its good points and its bad points. The good? You're pumped up to do your best. The bad? You're afraid to fail, and failure is part of every game.

As soon as the buyer said "you're it!" I did not see myself standing before millions of viewers—maybe as many as 60 million, mind you. No, I did not see all those people. In a flash, all I saw was one huge face in that painting staring at me: my dad.

Predictably, after my first appearance, the very first phone call was from guess who? Dad!

Dad had some comments about my delivery, and what's really frustrating about Dad is this: As in most cases, all his comments were right on target. For example, as politely but directly as possible, he let me know that while my camera presence was effective, I had apparently overtrained and was much too technical during my presentation.

"You used too many big words," he said. "You went on too much about features versus benefits."

Too much detail, he maintained—correctly—tends to dilute the message.

Although at that moment I wasn't prepared to hear his comments—after all, the product was a top-selling item on Q2—somewhere deep down I knew he was right, and I incorporated his wisdom into my future on-air appearances.

Once it hit me that this was it, that I was to be an on-air spokesperson for Lite Bites, I did everything in my power to be fully prepared so that I could explain my story to QVC viewers in layman's terms.

Here's what I mean by layman's terms: I asked the creators of Lite Bites why a particular herb was used in Lite Bites. Their enthusiastic answer took up a good half hour. That was just one herb and there are seven more herbs and nutrients, plus 22 vitamins, minerals, and other ingredients to boot!

I faced the task of reducing all this information, which could take hours, into just ten minutes of airtime, while still telling my story. Here's where I first learned the importance of talking in the language of benefits. That is, benefits as opposed to features and technical detail.

Why do Lite Bites products do so well on QVC? I am the benefit of the benefit. By this I mean that by demonstrating my weight loss and fitness through Lite Bites, I am a walking, talking billboard for the products.

As a prospective vendor, keep this in mind. Your spokesperson's relationship to the product is key.

A month before airtime, I started getting jittery. By this time, I had pretty much nailed my presentation. I spent hours with Dean and Cheryl Radetsky going over each and every herb and learning how each herb works alone and together with the others. I also spent hours reading books on herbs, vitamins, and minerals, and to make myself as knowledgeable as possible, I even took a crash course in human biology and nutrition.

On that score, I was ready. I was ready with the facts about Lite Bites.

But was I ready to perform on TV?

In preparing for the new event, I bought new clothing, got my hair cut, and had my nails done.

This last item deserves some explanation. I remember being at many a family dinner and hearing my father comment about the condition of a particular show host's fingernails. Yes, fingernails, and yes, Dad was quite emphatic! As a matter of fact, when I met my producer at QVC for the first time—Craig Adler, who'd been at the station from day one—he shook my hand and said, "How are your finger-nails? I'm sure your father has already cautioned you."

So there you have it—I got a manicure. That was a tougher assignment than you might think because I had to learn to stop biting my nails.

That was just the beginning. As I mentioned earlier, Dad copied me on a series of do's and don'ts memos that he had sent to QVC show hosts over the years. I quoted from these memos in a previous chapter. He suggested I read these memos to make sure that I didn't make the same mistakes. I found it interesting that a number of show hosts, in partic-ular Kathy Levine, one of my favorites, were doing some of the things my dad had cautioned me against—like talking with people on the set who were off camera. And yet these hosts were enormously successful. (My dad's response: "Well, that's Kathy!")

There is no such thing as a perfect show. That's one of the problems my father faced when he decided to go on-air himself with the Le Mirador skin care line. The line was created from the products that won the First International Skincare Competition, which was sponsored by the Swiss spa that he then owned. He tried to make it a perfect show. He actually tried to script it down to the last detail and wanted to limit the number of on-air phone calls. But is there any fun in being perfect? No. The risk of a little imper-fection is what keeps us on our toes, keeps us laughing, and keeps the QVC viewer from expecting robots rather than fallible human beings. After several appearances on QVC, Dad felt that his focus on technical details was impairing his ability to be a charismatic spokesperson, so he decided to stop appearing personally. Even so, the Le Mirador skin care line is one of the top five reordered products on QVC, right behind Lite Bites bars! After I've been on-air, Dad often calls me up and ask how my dollars per minute were, that is, how many dollars of inventory were sold every minute I was on the air. Those calls keep me on my toes— and my presentations have the same effect on him. It's ironic how life turns some situations completely around—in this case, a family relationship that was always a challenge for me and is now competitive in the best sense of the word!

I should stop here to remind you that for openers I was to start as an on-air guest on Q2, QVC's sister channel, which at the time was broadcasting live from New York. Fortunately or unfortunately, unlike most first-time guests, my opening round was not limited to just one on-air appearance. At Q2, I appeared eight times that first day as the "New Year's Resolution Item of the Day." I had to work with eight different show hosts. That was quite a challenge because show hosts vary in personality and energy levels and, as a guest, it's your job to adjust.

I got more experience in one day than most on-air guests get in a year.

Before going on-air for the first time, you should watch QVC to study how your show host interacts with other guests.

Always ask your buyer which show host you are scheduled to be working with. You should also ask when he or she will be on-air the day of your appearance. This second question is important because the show host may be going on-air before you arrive. In that case, you would be unable to talk to the host before you go on-air. That would not be the worst thing to happen. These show hosts are pros, and they are all great at what they do. But it might make you more at ease to meet them ahead of airtime. When your buyer notifies you of your first air date, make sure you ask when the show host first goes on-air so that you can be there ahead of time.

If you'd like to know when your show host is appearing, log on to QVC's home page at www.qvc.com. Under the program guide, you'll find the show titles listed along with the show host's schedules.

Always expect the unexpected and be prepared for it. Be prepared for anything! When I was making that first appearance on Q2, I was walking back to the Green Room when someone turned a corner while carrying a cup of coffee. We bumped into each other and some of it spilled onto my pants. That's why it's important to bring extra clothing. (I get kidded that I bring more clothes than Joan Rivers.)

After makeup that first time, I was escorted down to the studio where some stranger started putting his hand down my shirt and routing wires around my body. One of these wires was for a wireless mike, the other for the IFB. IFB stands for interrupted feedback. This is how the producers talk to you in your ear while you're on-air.

If you are a first-time on-air guest, the producer won't say much to you over the IFB, since it's distracting. But you'll likely be told that a videotape is ready to run, or that you should redemonstrate the product, or that you should turn to a certain camera.

Wearing an IFB has to be one of life's stranger experiences. Someone can be talking to you while you are in the middle of a conversation with the show host or a caller. Your first reaction is to turn to that side, since the sound is coming through one ear. Staying focused while being interrupted, that's something you learn with experience— experience that had better come fast.

After you get some experience dealing with IFB, the producers will actually tell you jokes while you're on the air. It becomes part of the whole experience and can be a lot of fun.

It's now showtime! I've had a brief introduction with my show host. We're sitting in front of the cameras. There's a river of sweat rolling down my back, which makes me worry whether the wireless mike and IFB are waterproof. Meaning—am I in for the shock of my life?

Now we're live. About five minutes into the presentation, I look at the time remaining and think, I'll never be able to talk this long about Lite Bites. The next thing I know, the 12 minutes are up and I didn't cover all there was to present.

That first experience taught me this lesson—as I've already stated, there is no such thing as the perfect show. For example, the charts that I used that first time were excessive, in a word, overkill. What did work was this: the fact that I came on as an average guy.

In the end, Lite Bites was the top-selling item of the day. I will always be grateful to Melissa Radin, the buyer at Q2 who held my hand throughout those first-day jitters.

Of course, there is no limit to learning how to best present your product. I'm always open to suggestions.

Based on my years of experience at QVC, here are my top ten tips for going on-air at QVC, whether it's the first time or hundredth time:

1. All show hosts use blue cards. These cards have very technical descriptions of your product. I suggest that you make up your own blue cards with your QVC-approved key selling benefits. (See the samples on pages 164–165.)

2. Bring extra clothes—someone might spill coffee on you before airtime.

3. QVC asks you to arrive two hours before the start of your show—BE THERE!

4. Bring extra samples of your product when size permits.

5. Bring extra copies of any graphic support material or videotapes that may be used on-air.

6. Dress appropriately for your product and your presentation. (Don't wear a suit and tie if you're demonstrating a piece of exercise equipment.)

7. Check the show title on iQVC (www.qvc.com). On the program guide, as noted above, you will see when the show starts. Make the connection to your product. Better yet, check your show host's schedule with your buyer and find out when the host starts his or her shift. Try to meet the show host before your airtime. You should also watch your show host prior to your airtime so that you get the feel of his or her personality. All hosts are different.

8. One week prior to your appearance, FedEx a copy of your on-air blue card and a product sample (if possible) to your show host. This should be accompanied by a cover letter that explains what you would like to discuss on-air, or what has worked in the past regarding the product.

9. Bring along a blank videotape, so that you'll be able to tape your show directly from the Green Room.

10. If possible, have someone accompany you so that this individual can monitor the total phone calls that come into QVC at every two-minute interval while you are on-air. This is important because, while watching the tape later on, you'll be able to see what parts of your presentation piqued the interest of the QVC viewer. You will also see what did not work. When phone call

activity goes down, that means the viewer lost interest. You may have had a great product, but the message did not connect with the QVC viewer

Do I still get the jitters before going on-air? I call it energy. You need to be a little nervous to charge yourself up. Then there's the fact that you're going to be on live. That's always risky, but it's also part of the fun.

Chapter Ten

Luck, Timing, and Life: Finding Your Way to the Green Room

How do you find QVC's Green Room? It's something like that joke about finding your way to Carnegie Hall. "Practice, practice." In QVC's case, it's a matter of following the tips and tricks on product positioning offered in this book.

These are your directions to the Green Room.

So far you've passed the major checkpoints. Your initial presentation was on target. Your first meeting with a buyer was persuasive and to the point. You've presented and positioned your product properly. You've followed up diligently without being a pain in the backside. Your product obviously passed QVC's tough Quality Assurance standards.

How to get to the Green Room? Well, it's not easy. It's strategically and logistically tucked away, because QVC does not want the general public wandering in. The Green Room is for guests and those directly involved with the show. Best not to bring family and friends.

When you enter QVC's main lobby you register with Security and they will arrange for someone to escort you to the Green Room. The only exception may be if you're a regular guest and know your way around. Security will still issue you a badge, but then you're on your own.

There may be other issues concerning props and bulky supplies. Those needs should be coordinated through your producer.

Now you're ready to go on-air.

The Green Room is the staging area for on-air guests, replete with light refreshments and places to get changed. There is also pleasant chatter among guests like yourself.

The chitchat is great, but be careful what you say. You don't know who's involved with what product, and a critical comment may wound somebody's feelings. I've seen it happen.

Admittedly, everyone, even stars, are nervous, since this is make-or-break time.

On my first visit to the Green Room, I was about as green as anyone could be. I was nervous and didn't know what to expect. This was at Q2 and I knew nothing except this: I had a great product, Lite Bites Wafers, and a great story, two of the key elements needed for a successful presentation.

But confident as I was, was there a chance that I might bomb?

So there I am, waiting for about an hour before my first shot on-air, and believe me, I was sweating.

The rest, of course, is history.

Your first visit to the Green Room will probably be no different from mine. You will have the comfort of good company, since others will be sharing your anxiety. In Green Rooms Q and V, you will typically be with other vendors and on-air spokespersons much like yourself. You should find that the more experienced guests will lend you a hand and give you advice if you ask.

Life in QVC's Green Room can be a tremendous learning experience. By paying attention to the dynamics of the Green Room, you can try to figure out why the good products did well, and why the poor products did poorly.

Let me explain what I mean. There are a series of computer screens in the Green Room. One tallies the sales of each product. The other keeps track of the volume of phone calls. I find the phone activity screen to be the most valuable in determining what makes a QVC viewer become a QVC buyer. This is so because you can watch in real time what aspects of the show make the QVC viewer pick up the phone.

Be a fly on the wall while you're in the Green Room. Listen and observe. See what the host or guest does that makes the phones light up.

Another thing about the Green Room, you never know who you're going to meet there. One of my most pleasant experiences in the Green Room was running into George Hamilton back when I was still a rookie on the job. I walked in, and there was this movie star reading a newspaper, and eating a Lite Bites bar. Made my day! I introduced myself and found him to be totally unaffected. A true gentleman.

This leads me to Tim Conway and Harvey Korman. They were real team players. Both comedians were there to present one of their videotapes. They were on the set, ready to go on-air, when Tim Conway caught sight of my Big Marv —that's the lifesize cut-out of me when I weighed over three hundred pounds.

"What's that!" Conway gasped.

I said, "That was me three years ago before Lite Bites."

"I want a box of that," Conway said, and I was happy to deliver.

Next thing I know, I'm on the air in the middle of my presentation looking for my oversized pants and jacket, part of my demonstration, when I hear laughter coming from all corners of the set.

Did I say something funny?

No, it was Tim Conway and Harvey Korman.

They came walking onto my set, Harvey with his shirt opened up and his belly sticking out, followed by Tim Conway wearing my old jacket and old pants, and eating a Lite Bites bar.

Naturally, the pants were too big and they fell to the floor.

Tim, while eating the Lite Bites bar, quipped: "Look, these things really work!"

To me this demonstrated the great camaraderie that exists at QVC.

That good-natured spirit is something you'll often find in the Green Room. When you're doing well, there tends to be a lot of high-fives and congratulations, and if you're not doing well, you'll find others there to offer consolation.

We also help each other. The person next to you will gladly insert your videocassette into the recorder if you're by yourself. Another vendor may help you take notes as to what may or may not have happened to the phone lines while you were on the air.

I even met my future publisher, Esther Margolis, in the Green Room. She was there in connection with another book her company, Newmarket Press, was publishing—Suze Orman's first book, *You've Earned It, Don't Lose It*—which became, as many of you know, one of QVC's greatest success stories. Just like me, Suze was given her first opportunity to present her product on Q2, which Esther recalls took many months of calls and convincing and a pre-interview with Suze before the buyer would gamble on a first-time author of a personal finance book. Suze was an immediate hit, which led to more bookings on Q2, and later on QVC. Esther accompanied Suze during her QVC visits, which was lucky for me. When Esther heard my story, she seemed impressed and quite earnestly told me, "You've got a book in you." Well, as you've learned in these pages and as Esther now knows, when presented with a challenge like that, I don't rest until I've accomplished whatever it is I need to do. And you are holding the results of that challenge right now in your hands!

So there's a lot of rooting, cheering, sharing of information, and commiserating in the Green Room.

Now, I keep speaking about the Green Room, when actually there are three.

Green Rooms Q and V handle multiple guests and tend to have a higher energy because of the number of people.

Green Room C is reserved for private or special needs, such as guests who require the Green Room all day. This would likely be a Today's Special Value Guest. Green Room C will also be made available for guests who are accompanied by a large support staff.

When you arrive at QVC, the pages will assign you to an appropriate Green Room.

Another word or two about Green Room etiquette. The chairs in front of the computer screens—which I refer to as the Chairs of Honor—belong exclusively to those vendors whose products are being presented on-air at that moment. There's no rule about this, merely common courtesy.

Yes, there's a lot to learn in the Green Room by being a fly on the wall. But it's also expected that you give others their space and be respectful of their need to listen carefully to their show while it's being broadcast.

The Green Room is really where you do business. It's where you analyze your sales, and it's where you hopefully develop lasting relationships.

When you walk into QVC's Green Rooms you will see stars and those who act like stars. As you're developing your relationship with QVC, remember who the customer is. It is QVC. Your appearance on-air does not make you a star. The performance of your product will determine how soon you see the Green Room again.

Thinking about the Green Room and how I came to write this book brings me back to the mantra I live by: Luck, Timing, and Life. Who knew that Big Marvin, the photographer-mole, the real estate mogul (well, that's stretching it a bit!), one of the youngest pilots ever to get licensed to fly Lear Jets, would end up back in the Green Room and on TV, 80 pounds slimmer, productive, confident, and enormously happy? By every standard I can think of, my life has been a success. Did I ever think I'd be saying something like that? Did I plan to go on-air and be a product representative for Lite Bites? There was a time in my life when I thought all I ever wanted to do was fly airplanes. And I probably could have made a nice living doing that. But would that have been the real Marv Segel? Perhaps. Perhaps not. I'll never know.

I'll never know, because life presented me with a series of challenges, a set of opportunities, and I decided to find out where those opportunities would lead me. There are those who might say that I had a series of lucky breaks that most people don't get. But I believe that most people don't understand the lucky breaks that are presented to them every day. They are not easy to recognize. Did I recognize those challenges as lucky breaks at the time? Absolutely not. I had to take risks—well-thought-out risks, to be sure—but risks nonetheless. It was not easy to walk away from a 15-year career in real estate to pursue the makers of a rather tiny energy bar. It took even more guts to turn down that $75,000 job in the field I had just left at a time when I had no real income. But these are the kinds of challenges that we all face every single day. The difference between someone like me, who others may think of as lucky, and those who never seem to have good luck is this: The ability to recognize that those challenges can only be turned into luck if you are willing to change the way you've always conducted your life.

It doesn't really matter what the challenges are. You may need to lose 20 pounds or 120 pounds. You may need to leave one job and go to another, or start your own business, or ask for that raise and promotion. Your challenges may be altogether different: reaching out to a long-lost relative or mending torn fences with your next-door neighbor. You may be facing important challenges to the maintenance of your health quite apart from any need or desire to lose weight. Whatever your challenges are, it helps to recognize them as opportunities for change. When you look back on those opportunities, you'll know whether you met the requirement for change and what the results have been.

I have never regretted any of the experiences I've had. Some weren't pleasant—my life as a photographer in that dark basement at the Franklin Mint was no joy—yet that job helped me later in life when I had to think quickly on my feet about how to reposition a floundering Lite Bites product. I've always believed that these challenges will eventually be viewed as the *luck* I needed at just the right *time* to change my *life*.

If you think about your life—what has happened to you and what you can predict—you'll be amazed at the courage you've shown already. Perhaps you've married and have had children. You can think of those events in your life as your biggest strokes of luck. Even picking up the phone and ordering this book or finding it in a bookstore was an opportunity for you to change that you faced and have accepted. Some people would not have been able to find this book, either because of lethargy or an attitude that won't recognize opportunity and the need for change. As you look back on your life, I'm sure you can find lots of examples of the path you took and the ones you didn't. Each one of those decisions has brought you to this point in your life.

My hope is that by sharing a bit more of my luck, the timing, and the details of my life that I will have inspired you to take a good, long look at your own situation. Perhaps now that you've made the connection between opportunity and change, you'll know exactly what you need to do to bring some luck into your own life at exactly the right time. When you do, you'll find the way to your own "Green Room," that place in your life that represents success, however you define it.

I hope my father realizes how much I love him and respect him and have valued his guidance through the years. His business ethics have always been and still are impeccable and second to none. That's a quality I have always admired in him and hope that I emulate every single day. As we've grown older (and I've grown up), I think we've grown wiser to the ways of the other and understand each other more with every passing day. He was always supportive of my efforts to succeed; now that I have, on my own terms, I realize we share many common values and traits that successful people possess, and I appreciate those traits now as I never did before. When I was still a novice, certain things he did puzzled me. It's amazing to me how I see him now and truly understand—and accept—what makes us the men we are today.

You've read about my life and I'm just as interested in reading about yours. Let me hear about your successes and your struggles. You can write me at QVC. I wish you all good luck, good timing, and a long and productive life.

Part Four

The Lite Bites® Healthy Lifestyle Workbook

The Lite Bites Healthy Lifestyle Workbook[1]

This workbook is a tool to help you get the most out of your commitment to develop a healthy lifestyle using the Lite Bites Fat-Fighting System. Feel free to photocopy the pages that interest you, motivate you, challenge you to keep your interest in and commitment to a new healthy lifestyle. The workbook is structured using the four-step plan outlined in Chapter 6 of this book. The plan's four steps include two for your head (Planning and Attitude) and two for your body (Food and Fitness) and the workbook is structured the same way. The goal is to provide you with information and activities that will keep you focused on the job ahead.

PLANNING

My Personal Strategy for Losing Weight

Think about your day, each and every day. Plan each day's meals to get balanced nutrition. If today is a special day and the celebration involves food, be sure to plan today's other meals so that you don't consume more calories than you are expending.

---

[1] The material in this workbook is based on the Lite Bites program developed by Optimum Lifestyle, Inc. and used by permission. Copyright © 1998 by Optimum Lifestyle, Inc. All rights reserved.

What are today's mealtime options?

Breakfast _____

Lunch _____

Dinner _____

Special Events
(Birthday, Holiday,
Special Events
with Friends, etc.) _____

What are my healthy lifestyle goals?

Weight _____

Dress Size _____

Necessary Weight Loss/Gain_____

Fitness Level _____

Other Goals:

    Short Term _____

    Long Term _____

How committed am I to living more healthfully? Describe.

_____

_____

_____

_____

My top three goals for this month are:

1. _____

2. _____

3. _____

Review these three goals first thing every morning.

My non-food reward for achieving these goals are:

1. _____

2. _____

3. _____

(Non-food rewards could be getting a pedicure or seeing a movie you've wanted to see. Be good to yourself. You deserve it.)

FOOD
First tackle fat, then tackle portion control.

Fat

At your local bookstore, grocery, or health food store, buy a fat gram counter and keep track of your fat grams with the help of this handy chart. You should also read the nutritional labels of every food product you eat to determine exactly how much fat and how many calories you are consuming. See chapter six to determine how many calories you need to consume every day.

Reading every nutritional label of the foods you eat, keep track of the fat grams you consume every day.

	Food	**# of Fat Grams**
Breakfast		
Lunch		
Dinner		
Snacks		

Cutting Fat from My Diet

Instead of _____, I can try _____.

Instead of _____, I can try _____.

Instead of _____, I can try _____.

Instead of _____, I can try _____.

Instead of _____, I can try _____.

Instead of _____, I can try _____.

```
SOME SMART SWAPS
```

Instead of:	Have:	You save:
French Fries (3 oz.)	Baked Potato (med.)	14 g fat
Potato Chips (2 oz.)	Pretzel (2 oz.)	18 g fat
Ice Cream (1/2 cup)	Fruit Sorbet (1/2 cup)	7 g fat
Creamy Italian Dressing (1tbsp.)	Fat-Free Dressing (1 tbsp.)	8 g fat
Caesar Salad	Green Salad w/ fat-free dressing and grilled skinless chicken	30 g fat
Chocolate Croissant	Lite Bites Bar	27 g fat

Portion Control

Portion control is an acquired skill. Try these tips for re-educate your eyes (and stomach!).

1 cup pasta = closed fist
3 oz. protein = deck of cards
1 oz. popcorn = 4 handfuls
1 oz. potato chips = 2 handfuls
1 bagel = 2–4 slices bread, depending on size of bagel
Restaurant portion of pasta or protein= 2–3 servings
(Make use of doggy bags!)

The 1/3 Rule

A balanced meal consists of a plate that is 1/3 filled with protein and 2/3 filled with vegetables, grains, and fruit.

Creating Your Own Eating Plan

Make copies of the following chart to help you plan your daily food intake. They will help you remember what you've eaten and what you still need to take in each day for proper, balanced nutrition.

Today's Eating Journal

Today's Date: _____

My Top Healthy Lifestyle Goal for This Week: _____

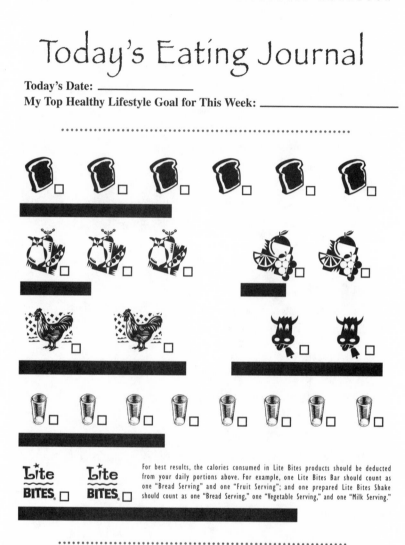

For best results, the calories consumed in Lite Bites products should be deducted from your daily portions above. For example, one Lite Bites Bar should count as one "Bread Serving" and one "Fruit Serving"; and one prepared Lite Bites Shake should count as one "Bread Serving," one "Vegetable Serving," and one "Milk Serving."

Today I felt... ☐ **great,** ☐ **okay,** ☐ **fat, or** ☐ _____

My hunger and cravings were... ☐ **under control, or** ☐ **wild & ravenous.**

What I could do better tomorrow is...

_____

_____

FITNESS

Before beginning any fitness program, check with your doctor. Your fitness program depends on how active you have been up to this point. If you've been a couch potato, then it is not realistic for you to start training for the marathon. It may simply be enough for you, at first, to take a walk every evening after dinner. Then increase your walks to once after each meal. Then increase the length of time you walk, the challenge of the terrain, etc. Listen to your body. It's made to move, it wants to move, and it will tell you when you're ready for the next fitness challenge.

Here are some fitness activities I can easily start this week (after I check with my doctor):

_____

_____

_____

_____

_____

_____

_____

ATTITUDE

Develop your own personal Conscious Eating Plan.

How to Develop Your Conscious Eating Plan

Follow these steps every time you think you are hungry—you'll be amazed at the results.

- Before eating anything, take a deep breath while counting to four. Hold it to the count of four. Now exhale to the count of four. Do this four times. This exercise will help you "be in the moment," instead of unconsciously inhaling an entire plate of food without even "checking in" to find out what you really need to eat (if anything).

- Now ask yourself this question and be honest with your answer: "Am I hungry?" If your answer is yes, ask yourself, "What for?" Food? Or something else, like connection with someone? Or relief from boredom? Become aware that hunger isn't just for food.

- If it is for food, ask "What will satisfy me?" By following your "internal cues," you will be able to truly feel satisfied by what you choose to eat.

- Now eat s-l-o-w-l-y. Taste each bite. Chew each mouthful, paying attention to all of the sensations. Stay present with the act of eating.

- Notice when you are beginning to feel full, and STOP EATING.

When I'm stressed, instead of mindless munching, I can do the following:

    1. _____

    2. _____

    3. _____

The times I use food to cope with feelings are:

    1. _____

    2. _____

    3. _____

    I will instead do the following:

    1. _____

    2. _____

    3. _____

The times I use food as a Great Escape are:

    1. _____

    2. _____

    3. _____

    I will instead do the following:

    1. _____

    2. _____

    3. _____

Examples of my own personal All-or-Nothing Thinking are:

1. _____

2. _____

3. _____

I will instead do the following:

1. _____

2. _____

3. _____

My binge triggers are:

1. _____

2. _____

3. _____

Other unconscious cues to eat are:

1. _____

2. _____

3. _____

I will instead do the following:

1. _____

2. _____

3. _____

FOOD DIARY

Keeping track of your daily food triggers will help you keep your consumption of food under control. Create your own food diary or use the one below. If you find you're eating a pizza (or two) every time you feel anxious, or you tend to feel tired and sluggish after you have the "usual" for lunch, you can experiment with other strategies to find what will work better.

Day & Date	Time	What I Ate...	How I Felt...

Day & Date	Time	What I Ate...	How I Felt...

Day & Date	Time	What I Ate...	How I Felt...

Day & Date	Time	What I Ate...	How I Felt...

Day & Date	Time	What I Ate...	How I Felt...

Day & Date	Time	What I Ate...	How I Felt...

Day & Date	Time	What I Ate...	How I Felt...

Day & Date	Time	What I Ate...	How I Felt...

Day & Date	Time	What I Ate...	How I Felt...

Day & Date	Time	What I Ate...	How I Felt...

Index